QUESTION BANK

Vol 2

JAR-FCL
Type Examples

Pooleys Flight Equipment Ltd
Elstree Aerodrome Herts UK
Telephone 0208 953 4870
Facsimile   0208 953 5219

QUESTION BANK

Vol 2

by Anthony Stevens

Aviation Law

Navigation General

Radio Navigation

Meterology

Electrics

Human Performance & Limitations

Operational Procedures

Communications

Preface

This book contains over 500 sample questions with answers for the JAR-FCL Type Example, Theoretical Knowledge exam papers and is supplemented by Volume 1 to cover the full syllabus.

The questions are based on the published learning objectives and are representative of the format and degree of difficulty that students will face in the actual exams and are designed to give as broad a coverage as possible of the different subjects. Furthermore, they have been written by an approved ground instructor using guidelines from the appropriate authorities.

The questions contained in this book will be updated at regular intervals to keep pace with any changes or additions to the JAR-FCL requirements.

The author and publisher of this book and its complimentary volumes wish all students good luck with their training process particularly at a time of significant change within the aviation industry.

Anthony Stevens

CONTENTS

NAVIGATION PAPER ONE

1. For a runway direction of 160(M) and a surface wind of 090(M)/40kt, the cross-wind component and direction of drift is:

    (a) 38kt right
    (b) 14kt right
    (c) 21kt right
    (d) 38kt left

2. An aircraft requires a minimum head wind component of 10kt and has a cross wind limit of 25kt. With runway 22 in use and surface wind direction of 270(M) what min and max wind speeds are acceptable?

    (a) 10kts and 25kts
    (b) 32kts and 16kts
    (c) 6kts and 40kts
    (d) 16kts and 32kts

3. An aircraft follows the 30S parallel of latitude. The route followed is a:

    (a) Great Circle
    (b) Minimum Time Route
    (c) Rhumb Line
    (d) Small circle

4. The Great Circle distance from A 4700N 3230W to B at 4700N 14730E is:

    (a) 7366nm
    (b) 5160nm
    (c) 2580nm
    (d) 7895nm

5. The Rhumb Line distance from A to B in question 4 is:

    (a) 5160nm
    (b) 7895nm
    (c) 10800nm
    (d) 7366nm

6. At the end of evening civil twilight on August 11th at 03500S 11630W, the Local Mean Time and local date at 01200N 09315E is:

    (a) 0751   12th August
    (b) 0138   12th August
    (c) 0751   11th August
    (d) 1925   11th August

7. A flight is planned from Gander, Newfoundland (4857N 5434W) to arrive at Nice (4340N 0715E) at 0900 Standard Time on May 5th. If the flight time is 6hr 15min, the LMT and local date of departure from Gander are:

(a) 0145   May 5th
(b) 2207   May 4th
(c) 0523   May 5th
(d) 2215   May 4th

8. On a Transverse Mercator chart earth convergency is correctly represented:

(a) At all points on the chart
(b) At the parallel of origin
(c) At the poles and the equator
(d) At the meridian of tangency

9. A Great Circle track is drawn between 3500N 02300W (A) and 0700N 00400E (B). The initial track is measured as 110(T). The initial track for the return flight from B to A would be:

(a) 299.5(T)
(b) 290(T)
(c) 119.5(T)
(d) 294(T)

10. If the aircraft continued its flight beyond B to C, what would the Rhumb Line track measured at B?

(a) 110(T)
(b) 119.5(T)
(c) 295(T)
(d) 115(T)

11. On a Lamberts Conformal Chart scale is correct .... and earth convergency is correctly represented ....

(a) At the parallel of origin   at the standard parallels
(b) At the standard parallels   at the equator
(c) At the standard parallels   at the parallel of origin
(d) At the parallel of origin   at the parallel of origin

12. On a Lamberts chart the convergency factor is 0.815.
The parallel of origin is:

(a) 3530N
(b) 5436N
(c) 5500N
(d) 39N

13. If you use a Polar Stereographic chart to plot a flight from A to B, at the point when the route passes closest to the pole the true track will be:

   (a)   090
   (b)   090 or 270
   (c)   270
   (d)   180

14. Using the Air Almanac the lowest latitude in June when there is no sunset at sea level is:

   (a)   66N
   (b)   68N
   (c)   72N
   (d)   62N

15. The scale of a Mercator chart is 1:4,500,000 at latitude 36N. At latitude 25S the scale is:

   (a)   1:4,500,000
   (b)   1:3,250,000
   (c)   1:5,040,000
   (d)   1:6,000,000

A straight line is drawn on a polar stereographic chart from A (82N 60W) to B (82N 150E). Using this information answer questions 16 to 18.

16. The true track measured at A is:

   (a)   165
   (b)   330
   (c)   195
   (d)   345

17. The track measured at B is:

   (a)   015
   (b)   195
   (c)   345
   (d)   165

18. The longitude at which the track angle will measure 270 is:

   (a)   135E
   (b)   45E
   (c)   135W
   (d)   45W

19. The spacing between the meridians of 10E and 20E on a mercator chart is 3.75 inches at 69N. The scale of the chart at 50N is:

(a) 1:7,500,000
(b) 1:4,200,000
(c) 1:9,000,000
(d) 1:2,500,000

20. A track is drawn on a lamberts chart between A and B in the southern hemisphere. The track measures 140(T) at the meridian through A and 128(T) at the meridian through B. Which of the following statements is correct:

(a) The rhumb line track from B to A is 314(T)
(b) Conversion angle is 12 degrees
(c) The great circle bearing of A from B is 314(T)
(d) The rhumb line track from A to B is 146 degrees

21. A line on a map joining places having zero magnetic variation is:

(a) An isogonal
(b) An aclinic line
(c) An isoclinal
(d) An agonic line

An aircraft has its automatic flight control system coupled to the outputs of the INS and is flying between waypoint 3 (45N 20W) and waypoint 4 (45N 30W). Using this information answer questions 22 to 25.

22. With DSR TK/STS selected on the CDU, the initial track readout between waypoints 3 and 4 is:

(a) 270
(b) More than 270
(c) Less than 270
(d) 090

23. Assuming no error in the INS, the ground distance between the two waypoints will be:

(a) 424.2 nm
(b) slightly more than 424.2 nm
(c) slightly less than 424.2 nm
(d) 600 nm

24. When the INS longitude indicates 25W, the latitude readout will be:

(a) north of 45N
(b) south of 45N
(c) 45N
(d) 35N

25. Assuming a constant drift, the aircraft true heading between the two waypoints would have:

(a)   remained constant
(b)   decreased by more than 10 degrees
(c)   increased by less than 10 degrees
(d)   decreased by less than 10 degrees

26. A land feature is observed 25 degrees to the left. The aircraft heading is 280(M) with variation 10E. The bearing (T) of the land from the aircraft is:

(a)   315
(b)   245
(c)   145
(d)   265

An aircraft is to climb from FL40 to FL 240 with a mean RAS of 200kt and mean rate of climb of 2000ft/min. Forecast winds and temperatures are:

FL40   240/20   +8c
FL240   280/40   -26c

27. The mean TAS for the climb is:

(a)   250kt
(b)   260kt
(c)   270kt
(d)   240kt

28. The flight time for the climb is:

(a)   20 mins
(b)   6 mins
(c)   10 mins
(d)   14 mins

29. Given: True track 125, TAS 180, true heading 115, GS 150kts; the W/V is:

(a)   153/42
(b)   076/42
(c)   256/42
(d)   076/30

30. PNR & CP are calculated for a flight using an average fuel flow and TAS and a forecast wind component. CP is closer to destination than to departure point. If the aircraft holds over a navigation beacon for a short time after take-off, the effect on the distance to CP/PNR will be:

(a)   No effect on CP, PNR distance reduced
(b)   No effect on either CP or PNR
(c)   CP & PNR distance reduced
(d)   CP distance unchanged, PNR distance increased

31. An aircraft is flying from A to B 250nm away with a required track of 305(T). The initial heading is 315(M) with variation 2E. The expected drift is:

    (a)   12 starboard
    (b)   8 port
    (c)   8 starboard
    (d)   12 port

32. After 25 minutes flying a fix puts the aircraft on a bearing of 307(M) from A at a range of 150nm. The groundspeed is:

    (a)   240kts
    (b)   360kts
    (c)   300kts
    (d)   270kts

33. Using the information in question 32 what immediate alteration of heading is required to fly to B?

    (a)   4 degrees port
    (b)   6 degrees port
    (c)   10 degrees port
    (d)   10 degrees starboard

34. A direct reading compass is subject to acceleration errors. These result in:

    (a)   The compass indicates a turn towards the equator
    (b)   The compass will lag behind the aircraft
    (c)   The compass indicates a turn towards the nearer pole
    (d)   The compass reading is not affected

35. A swing of the direct reading compass must be undertaken:

    (a)   After a change in electrical equipment or wiring
    (b)   After passing near a thunderstorm
    (c)   After a change in latitude of 10 degrees or more
    (d)   After flying on one heading for some time

36. Which of the following is an advantage of a Remote Reading Compass over a Direct Reading Compass:

    (a)   It does not suffer from acceleration errors
    (b)   It can provide heading information to other equipment
    (c)   It does not topple during violent manoeuvres
    (d)   It can be calibrated without the engines running

37. An aircraft is heading 288(C) with +4 deviation and where the variation is 22E. What are the true and magnetic headings respectively?

    (a)   306 and 284
    (b)   314 and 284
    (c)   270 and 292
    (d)   314 and 292

38. An aircraft is flying at a height of 1200ft in the circuit of an airfield with an elevation of 450ft. What clearance will the aircraft have over an aerial on the airfield if the aerial is 600ft amsl?

    (a)   600ft
    (b)   150ft
    (c)   1050ft
    (d)   1650ft

39. 12100 kgs/hour fuel flow with specific gravity 0.82 is also equivalent to:

    (a)   12270 litres/hour
    (b)   26600 lbs/hour
    (c)   3500 imperial gallons/hour
    (d)   4250 US gallons/hour

40. An aircraft is flying at 41000ft on a heading of 055(T) with variation of 5E. The OAT is ISA -10, W/V 360/50 and the aircraft is maintaining Mach 0.83. The track and groundspeed are:

    (a)   055(M) & 450kts
    (b)   060(M) & 440kts
    (c)   065(M) & 430kts
    (d)   055(M) & 440kts

NAVIGATION PAPER ONE - ANSWERS

1.	A	21.	D
2.	D	22.	B
3.	C	23.	C
4.	B	24.	A
5.	D	25.	D
6.	A	26.	D
7.	B	27.	A
8.	C	28.	C
9.	A	29.	B
10.	D	30.	A
11.	C	31.	D
12.	B	32.	B
13.	B	33.	C
14.	A	34.	C
15.	C	35.	A
16.	D	36.	B
17.	B	37.	D
18.	C	38.	C
19.	A	39.	B
20.	A	40.	D

1. The following symbol on a 1/2 million topographical chart represents;

    (a) A government heliport
    (b) A civil heliport
    (c) A hospital
    (d) A joint user heliport

2. Flying in the southern hemisphere the RMI reading from a VOR is 049. The earth convergency between the VOR and the aircraft's DR position is 6, magnetic variation at the VOR is 16E and at the aircraft is 12E. The bearing that should be plotted from the meridian through the VOR on a Mercator chart is:

    (a) 245
    (b) 248
    (c) 242
    (d) 229

3. The main use for the Oblique Mercator is:

    (a) To show rhumb lines correctly
    (b) To map countries with a large d. Long and a small d. Lat
    (c) To show major great circle routes accurately
    (d) To show N/S great circle routes only

4. For an observer on the ground in Hong Kong (2216N 11409E) the time of sunset (UTC) on July 22nd is:

    (a) 1108
    (b) 1845
    (c) 1045
    (d) 0959

5. The duration of evening civil twilight at Thule (6930N 05400W) on October 8th local date is:

    (a) 1 hour starting at 1753 LMT on the 8th
    (b) 1 hour starting at 0641 LMT on the 8th
    (c) 1 hour starting at 0541 LMT on the 8th
    (d) 1 hour starting at 1653 LMT on the 8th

6. When landing on runway 33 with a surface wind of 360/30:

    (a) The head wind component is 30kt
    (b) The drift is 15 degrees starboard
    (c) The cross wind component is 15kt from the right
    (d) The cross wind component is 26kt to the left

7. The meaning of the following aeronautical symbol is:

(a) A single obstacle, with lights, the top of which is 2450ft above ground level on ground 1160ft amsl

(b) Multiple obstacles, with lights, the tops of which are 2450ft amsl and 1160ft above the local ground level

(c) Multiple obstacles, with lights, whose tops are 2450ft amsl on high ground which is 1160ft amsl

(d) Multiple obstacles with tops 2450ft amsl and 1160ft above the local ground level

8. The UTC of sunset at LIMA, PERU (1202S 07707W) on August 12th is:

(a) 1757 UTC
(b) 2256 UTC
(c) 2330 UTC
(d) 2304 UTC

9. An aircraft heading 061(T) obtains a relative bearing from a NDB, whose longitude is 11 degrees different from the DR position and the mean latitude is 67N. Using a Lamberts chart with a parallel of origin of 52N, the bearing to plot from the meridian through the NDB is:

(a) 107.5
(b) 116
(c) 124.5
(d) 112

10. Using the information in question 9 the bearing to plot from the meridian through the NDB using a Polar Stereographic chart is:

(a) 107.5
(b) 116
(c) 105
(d) 127

11. An aircraft departs airfield A at 0200 UTC to fly to airfield B which is 350nm away at 180kts TAS. The planned track is 125(T) and initial heading 115(T). At 0220 UTC the aircraft's position is fixed 10nm left of track and 55nm from A. The W/V experienced since 0200 is:

(a) 105/16
(b) 126/16
(c) 175/36
(d) 046/16

12. Using the above information the immediate alteration at 0220 to make B is;

(a) 13 port
(b) 11 starboard
(c) 2 starboard
(d) 13 starboard

13. Using the information calculated in question 11, the ETA for B is:

(a)   0407 UTC
(b)   0341 UTC
(c)   0240 UTC
(d)   0358 UTC

14. An aircraft requires a minimum head-wind component of 10kt for take-off. The aircraft's cross-wind limit is 20kt. If the wind direction is 290(M) and the R/W in use is 25, the minimum and maximum wind to allow take-off are:

(a)   Min 10kts   Max 20kts
(b)   Min 10kts   Max 30kts
(c)   Min 13 kts   Max 30kts
(d)   Min 20kts   Max 30kts

15. A Lamberts chart has standard parallels of 30N and 40N. The distance measured along the 40N parallel between two points is 10cm. The distance measured along the 30N parallel between two points with the same change of longitude is:

(a)   8.8cm
(b)   10cm
(c)   11.3cm
(d)   12.8cm

16. The scale of a Mercator chart is 1:4,500,000 at 36N. The scale at 25S is:

(a)   1: 5,050,000
(b)   1: 4,500,000
(c)   1: 3,250,000
(d)   1: 6,000,000

17. PNR and CP are calculated for a flight using average fuel flow and TAS and forecast wind component. If the wind component is greater than forecast and the original CP was closer to destination than to departure airfield, the effect on the distance to CP/PNR will be:

(a)   CP distance increased   PNR distance increased
(b)   CP distance increased   PNR distance decreased
(c)   CP distance reduced   PNR distance reduced
(d)   CP distance reduced   PNR distance increased

18. On a Transverse Mercator chart scale is smallest at:

(a)   the projected pole
(b)   The equator
(c)   Outside a band 500nm from the central meridian
(d)   The central meridian

19. On a Lamberts chart the convergency between A (30N 10W) and B (45N 30W) is 12 degrees. If the rhumb line track from A to B is 314(T), the approximate great circle track from B to A is:

    (a)   128 (T)
    (b)   140 (T)
    (c)   122 (T)
    (d)   146 (T)

20. The standard time of sunrise at Oslo (5955N 01036E) on July 22nd is:

    (a)   0236
    (b)   0318
    (c)   0336
    (d)   0440

21. When transferring position lines to construct a 3 P/L fix having started a track plot from a DR position the parameters to be used are:

    (a)   Planned track and actual G/S
    (b)   Planned track and G/S
    (c)   TMG and actual G/S
    (d)   TMG and planned G/S

22. With reference to the earth's magnetic field, what is true of the Z component?

    (a)   It is the vertical direction of the earth's magnetic field
    (b)   It is the vertical component of the earth's magnetic field
    (c)   It is the horizontal component of the earth's magnetic field
    (d)   It reaches a maximum at the magnetic equator

23. Magnetic dip is:

    (a)   It is the angle between the compass needle and the horizontal
    (b)   It is the angle between the compass needle and the magnetic meridian
    (c)   It is the angle between the earth's magnetic field and the vertical
    (d)   It is the angle between the earth's magnetic field and the horizontal

24. What is the variation and deviation if the true, magnetic and compass headings are 355, 005 and 355 respectively:

    (a)   10W and 10W
    (b)   10E and +10
    (c)   10E and 10W
    (d)   10W and 10E

25. Sensitivity in a direct reading compass is achieved by:

(a) Reducing the moment of inertia by using several short powerful magnets instead of one long one
(b) By pendulous suspension
(c) By immersing the system in a liquid, thereby reducing their effective weight of the system on the pivot
(d) None of the above

26. With regard to a direct reading compass, turning errors:

(a)   Are maximum on north/south headings
(b)   Are maximum at the equator
(c)   Are maximum on east/west headings
(d)   Are zero at the poles

27. The position of the great circle between two points on the earth's surface relative to the rhumb line joining the same point is:

(a)   On the polar side in both hemispheres
(b)   On the equatorial side in the northern hemisphere
(c)   On the equatorial side in the southern hemisphere
(d)   On the polar side in the northern hemisphere only

28. An aircraft flying at 400km/hr consumes 3 US gallons/min on a flight of 630 statute miles. If the specific gravity is 0.85 the fuel used is:

(a)   3230 kgs
(b)   14620 lbs
(c)   1278 lbs
(d)   1465 kgs

29. On a Lamberts chart a straight line most closely represents a Great circle at:

(a)   At all points on the chart
(b)   The parallel of origin
(c)   The standard parallels
(d)   The equator

30. An aircraft passes over NDB A at 1234 intending to fly a true track of 087 with 155nm to VOR/DME B. TAS is 250kts and the true heading is 095. At 1243 the ADF indicates Relative Bearing of 192 to NDB A. At 1245 DME B indicates 100nm. Calculate the W/V experienced since 1234:

(a)   220/75
(b)   150/75
(c)   330/75
(d)   300/50

31. A DGI is free from random drift, uncorrected for latitude and stationary at latitude 52N. The effect of the earth's rotation on the indicated readings is:

(a)   Remain accurate
(b)   Increase at a rate proportional to Sin Lat
(c)   Decrease at a rate proportional to Cos Lat
(d)   Decrease at a rate proportional to Sin Lat

32. Movement of a gyroscope axis in the vertical plane is termed;

(a)   Drift
(b)   Topple
(c)   Precession
(d)   Wander

33. An aircraft is flying at FL 330 maintaining Mach 0.80 with a temperature deviation of ISA +10C. The TAS is:

(a)   475 kts
(b)   450 kts
(c)   463 kts
(d)   575 kts

34. The scale of a chart is 1:5,000,000 at 69N. If the scale of the chart is smaller than 1;5,000,000 at 75N, the projection being used is:

(a)   The Lambert
(b)   The Mercator
(c)   The Transverse Mercator
(d)   The Polar Stereographic

35. An aircraft is to fly from A to B, a distance of 1600nm at a TAS of 400kt. The endurance (excluding reserves) is 5 hours. The wind component that would put the CP between A & B in the same position as the PNR to A would be:

(a)   +80kt
(b)   -80kt
(c)   zero
(d)   +40kt

36. If there was a wind component of +15 from A to B, the distance from the CP to the PNR would be:

(a)   Zero
(b)   269nm
(c)   229nm
(d)   189nm

37. On a Polar Stereographic chart a straight line track is drawn between 70N 40W and 70N 160W. At its most northerly point this track will be:

(a) Exactly on 80n
(b) Just north of 80N
(c) Between 70N and 80N but closer to 80N
(d) Between 70N and 80N but closer to 70N

38. The distance between 10 degrees of longitude at 47N is represented on a chart by 5 inches. The scale of the chart is:

(a) 1:6,000,000
(b) 1:3,000,000
(c) 1:4,000,000
(d) 1:5,000,000

39. An aircraft in DR position 3200N 04000E obtains an RMI bearing from an NDB at 4400N 05000E of 042 degrees. If the variation at the DR position is 7E, the bearing to plot from the meridian through the NDB on a Lamberts chart is:

(a) 229(T)
(b) 049(T)
(c) 223(T)
(d) 235(T)

40. Using the above information the bearing to plot from the meridian through the NDB on a Mercator chart is:

(a) 229(T)
(b) 232(T)
(c) 226(T)
(d) 042(T)

NAVIGATION PAPER TWO - ANSWERS

1. A	21. B
2. B	22. B
3. C	23. D
4. A	24. A
5. D	25. C
6. C	26. A
7. B	27. A
8. D	28. D
9. A	29. B
10. C	30. C
11. B	31. D
12. D	32. B
13. A	33. A
14. C	34. D
15. C	35. B
16. A	36. C
17. B	37. C
18. D	38. A
19. A	39. D
20. C	40. B

1. The time of useful consciousness without oxygen at an altitude of 30000ft is:

    a.   2 - 3 minutes
    b.   15 - 30 seconds
    c.   30 seconds to 1 minute
    d.   30 minutes

2. A pilot is 5ft 9ins (175 cm) and weighs 78 kg. Based on BMI he is:

    a.   Overweight
    b.   Underweight
    c.   Within the normal range of body weights
    d.   Obese

3. Environmental stress can result from:

    a.   Failure to appreciate what is going on around you
    b.   Vibration, high or low relative humidity and noise
    c.   Perceived inability to get the job done
    d.   Noise and vibration only

4. A pilot carrying out an engine fire drill is exhibiting :

    a.   Instinctive behaviour
    b.   Skill based behaviour
    c.   Knowledge based behaviour
    d.   Rule based behaviour

5. By breathing 100% oxygen a partial pressure of oxygen within the lungs equivalent to MSL can be maintained up to:

    a.   40000ft
    b.   34000ft
    c.   30000ft
    d.   25000ft

6. The approximate percentage of oxygen in the atmosphere at 30000ft is:

    a.   40%
    b.   80%
    c.   10%
    d.   20%

7. The correct ascending order of stresses is said to be:

   a. Obtaining a mortgage, marriage, divorce, family death
   b. Family death, marriage, obtaining a mortgage, divorce
   c. Family death, divorce, marriage, obtaining a mortgage
   d. Marriage, family death, divorce, obtaining a mortgage

8. A longer than normal eyeball will result in the inability of the eye to focus on distant objects. This condition is:

   a. A stigmatism
   b. Hypermetropia or long sightedness.
   c. Myopia or short sightedness.
   d. Glaucoma.

9. If a crew member suffers any personal injury which results in incapacity to perform their flying duties he/she must inform the CAA:

   a. As soon as possible
   b. Within 7 days
   c. Within 3 weeks
   d. After 20 days

10. The use of drugs or tobacco to counter stress is known as:

    a. Action coping
    b. Symptom directed coping
    c. Cognitive coping
    d. Stress prevention

11. An essential feature of control design is that:

    a. Control size should relate to importance
    b. The shape should relate to the function
    c. The position of the control should relate to its function
    d. Controls should be standardised

12. Anthropometric data table measurements are taken from:

    a. The fifth to the ninety-fifth percentile, using both dynamic and static anthropometry
    b. The fifth to the ninety-fifth percentile, using dynamic anthropometry only
    c. The fiftieth percentile, using dynamic anthropometry only
    d. The average person , using static anthropometry only

13. The sympathetic nervous system provides the body with the immediate resources to react to a sudden source of stress. This is known as:

    a. The fight or flight syndrome
    b. Action coping
    c. The para-sympathetic reaction
    d. The fight or fright syndrome

14. The pupose of the Eustachian Tube is to:

    a.   Connect air pressure to the inner ear
    b.   Balance air pressure on both sides of the Cochlea
    c.   Balance air pressure on both sides of the ear drum
    d.   Connect ambient pressure to the outer ear

15. Damage to the ear drum or the ossicles can cause:

    a.   Otic barotrauma
    b.   Conductive deafness
    c.   Presbycusis
    d.   Noise Induced hearing loss

16. The function of an EEG is to:

    a.   Record the electrical activity of the brain.
    b.   Record the electrical activity of the heart muscle.
    c.   Monitor the blood pressure of the heart.
    d.   Monitor the blood pressure of the brain.

17. If you fly VFR from an airfield with runway width 45m to another airfield with runway width 27m, what possibility must be considered?

    a.   A high approach with undershoot
    b.   A low approach with overshoot
    c.   A high approach with overshoot
    d.   A low approach with undershoot

18. If you suffer a rapid decompression you should:

    a.   Select 100% oxygen and divert to the nearest suitable airfield
    b.   Descend to 10000 feet
    c.   Descend to 10000 feet or lower and use oxygen
    d.   Descend to 10000 feet and stop smoking

19. An aircraft accelerating in level flight may result in the pilot sensing:

    a.   Pitch down, contrary to the indications of an air driven artificial horizon
    b.   Pitch up, contrary to the indications of an air driven artificial horizon
    c.   Pitch up, supported by the indications of an air driven artificial horizon
    d.   Pitch up, supported by the indications of an air driven artificial horizon

20. Which of the following contributes most to maintaining spatial orientation:

    a.   Vision
    b.   Sense of balance
    c.   Vestibular system
    d.   Somato-sensory system

21. The possible symptoms of carbon monoxide poisoning are:

    a.   Anxiety, rapid breathing & dizziness
    b.   Lethargy, nausea, headache & ruddy complexion
    c.   Blueness of lips, impaired judgement and co-ordination
    d.   Excitability, tingling fingertips & loss of inhibition

22. A pilot suffering from gastro-enteritis is:

    a.   Fit to fly but only if taking medication
    b.   Fit to fly but only on a two pilot aeroplane
    c.   Unfit to fly unless taking medication and flying a two pilot aircraft
    d.   Unfit to fly regardless of any medication

23. An authoritarian type of person is likely to be:

    a.   A poor team leader but a compliant subordinate
    b.   Assertive in command and argumentative as a subordinate
    c.   A good team leader but ineffective as a subordinate
    d.   Autocratic and assertive both in command and as a subordinate

24. When in a high stress situation for a second time, having successfully dealt with it previously, a person's confidence & stress level would be:

    a.   Increased and increased
    b.   Decreased and increased
    c.   Increased and decreased
    d.   Decreased and decreased

25. If one's perception of the outside world is based on a mental model shaped by sensory information and experience, one tends to:

    a.   Give more weight to information that agrees with the model
    b.   Consider with equal weight all new information
    c.   Ignore all new information
    d.   Pay more attention to information that contradicts the model

26. What are the possible effects of hypoxia below 10000 feet?

    a.   None
    b.   Impaired mental agility only
    c.   Impaired mental agility below 5000 feet and night vision below 8000 feet
    d.   Impaired night vision below 5000 feet and mental agility below 8000 feet

27. If you look at a clear sky the eyes would focus on a point:

    a.   At infinity
    b.   1-2 metres ahead
    c.   10-20 centimetres ahead
    d.   250 metres ahead

28. Which of the following conditions causes the permanent denial of a flying licence?

    a.   Depression
    b.   Anxiety and phobic states
    c.   Obsessional disorders
    d.   Schizophrenia or manic depression

29. Air is drawn into the lungs by .... movement of the chest wall and .... movement of the diaphragm resulting in a .... of pressure in the chest.

a.	Downward	Outward	Rise
b.	Outward	Downward	Rise
c.	Outward	Downward	Fall
d.	Downward	Outward	Fall

30. The retinal size of an aircraft approaching on a collision course:

    a.   Remains the same as the aircraft approaches
    b.   Decreases at a uniform rate as the aircraft approaches
    c.   Increases at a very slow rate until shortly before impact
    d.   Increases at a uniform rate as the aircraft approaches

31. Errors in the application of skill based behaviour are most likely to occur to:

    a.   The experienced
    b.   The inexperienced
    c.   Both the experienced and the inexperienced
    d.   Those with no experience or limited experience

32. The working memory is able to:

    a.   Retain both acoustic and visual inputs equally
    b.   Retain acoustic inputs most easily
    c.   Retain visual inputs most easily
    d.   Retain acoustic and visual inputs equally but at different times

33. Haemoglobin is:

    a.   A product of respiration
    b.   Part of the bronchial tree controlled by the pulmonary vein
    c.   A specialist transport system for carbon dioxide found in red blood cells
    d.   A specialist transport system for oxygen found in red blood cells

34. A pilot who observes an aircraft accident will, in comparison to a member of the public:

    a.   Have stronger expectations about a likely set of events
    b.   Automatically discount any previous accident experience
    c.   Have a much better recollection of the basic events
    d.   Be a reliable witness at the accident investigation

35. Information in the working memory:

    a.   Is only retained for 4 to five minutes
    b.   Can be retained for long periods
    c.   Must be actively rehearsed to ensure long term retention
    d.   Is unaffected by the input of new information

36. Glass cockpits:

    a.   Can use a range of colour combinations providing that they are easy on the eye
    b.   Reduce the number of sources of information that the pilot must integrate
    c.   Provide a user friendly display that gives the pilot a good model of the real world
    d.   All of the above

37. Which of the following is not a source of toxic fumes?

    a.   Hydraulic fluid
    b.   Fuel vapour
    c.   Anti-icing fluid
    d.   None of the above

38. Hyperventilation:

    a.   Can result from an inadequate partial pressure of oxygen
    b.   Is unlikely to occur at high altitude
    c.   Is caused by having too little carbon monoxide in the blood
    d.   Is likely to result in death if not halted

39. Slow wave sleep:

    a.   Helps with learning and organisation and occurs early in the night
    b.   Restores the body physically and is mostly achieved late in the night
    c.   Restores the body and occurs early in the night
    d.   Helps with learning and organisation and occurs late in the night

40. A circular instrument with a fixed pointer and moving scale is:

    a.   A digital display instrument
    b.   An analogue display instrument
    c.   Poor for displaying engine RPM
    d.   Ideal for displaying range information

HUMAN PERFORMANCE AND LIMITATIONS 1 - ANSWERS

1. C		21. B	
2. A		22. D	
3. B		23. A	
4. D		24. C	
5. B		25. A	
6. D		26. D	
7. A		27. B	
8. C		28. D	
9. C		29. C	
10. B		30. C	
11. D		31. A	
12. A		32. B	
13. A		33. D	
14. C		34. A	
15. B		35. C	
16. A		36. B	
17. D		37. D	
18. C		38. A	
19. C		39. C	
20. A		40. B	

1. A runway which slopes upwards may induce a pilot to:

    a.   Make a shallow approach
    b.   Land short
    c.   Land long
    d.   Make a steep approach

2. If a pilot goes scuba diving to a depth of 30 feet, he/she should not fly within:

    a.   12 hours
    b.   36 hours
    c.   24 hours
    d.   48 hours

3. Which of the following is true?

    a.   The leans only occurs in IMC
    b.   The vestibular system alone produces reliable orientation stimuli
    c.   Vision is the most important sense for orientation
    d.   The leans only occur at night

4. A pilot is rostered for a duty that begins at 0830 UK local time. He/She flies a 10 hour sector to a destination where local time is +6 on UK local. After 24 hours rest a return sector of 10 hours is flown to the UK. The best rest pattern for this duty is:

    a.   Stay awake until 8 hours before call, then sleep
    b.   Sleep for 4 hours immediately and then for another 4 hours before the start of the second duty
    c.   Stay awake for a couple of hours, sleep for 4 hours, stay awake until 10 hours before call and then sleep
    d.   Keep in tune with your UK sleep pattern and supplement sleep before next duty

5. How many stages are there in a sleep cycle and how many cycles are to be expected in a normal night's sleep?

    a.   4 stages + REM   4-5 cycles
    b.   5 stages + REM   4-5 cycles
    c.   3 stages + REM   4-5 cycles
    d.   4 stages + REM   5-6 cycles

6. A group decision is likely to be .... than the average member's decision and .... than each individual member's decision:

    a.   Riskier   better
    b.   Worse   worse
    c.   Better   riskier
    d.   More cautious   better

7. The ideal professional pilot is:

    a.   "Person directed" rather than "goal directed"
    b.   Both "person" and "goal" directed
    c.   "Goal directed" rather than "person directed"
    d.   Neither "person" nor "goal" directed

8. A person who is aggressive and unpredictable is;

    a.   A stable extrovert
    b.   A stable introvert
    c.   An anxious introvert
    d.   An anxious extrovert

9. Grouping together all the instruments that relate to each engine:

    a.   Is not an important consideration for the design of a cockpit
    b.   Will make it more difficult to compare the performance of each engine
    c.   Will allow greater certainty when shutting down an engine
    d.   None of the above

10. Audio from the eardrum is passed to the inner ear by:

    a.   The vestibular system
    b.   The eustachian tubes
    c.   A network of small bones
    d.   The semi circular canals

11. A public transport pilot may use contact lenses to aid vision:

    a.   When a pair of suitable bifocal spectacles are carried for emergencies
    b.   Only during daylight
    c.   Only when VMC
    d.   Only during the cruise

12. An event that causes stress will:

    a.   Is unrelated to a person's perception of his own abilities
    b.   Have the same effect on all people
    c.   Will often occur without the individual realising
    d.   Have different effects on different people

13. Before making a non-urgent decision a good commander should:

    a.   Encourage questions and ideas before revealing their own
    b.   Reveal their own ideas first, then obtain those of the crew
    c.   Impose a decision on the crew
    d.   Discourage questions and ideas from the crew

14. "Environmental capture" is an:

    a.   Error during rule based behaviour
    b.   Error during knowledge based behaviour
    c.   Error during skill based behaviour
    d.   Occurrence when actions are repeated infrequently

15. When looking for a target in the distance one should;

    a.   Carry out a slow continuous scan
    b.   Use a succession of small, rapid eye movements
    c.   Keep your eyes still and only move your head
    d.   Select one point in space and concentrate on it for a long period

16. Depth perception is given by:

    a.   Colour, texture, size and relative movement
    b.   Colour, texture, size, relative movement in the near field & binocular vision for longer distances
    c.   Binocular vision alone
    d.   Binocular vision in the near field, with colour, texture, size & relative movement at longer distances

17. If a helicopter passenger feels unwell and is seated near to a window in direct or indirect sunlight, the required precautions are:

    a.   Move the passenger to a window seat so that the horizon is visible
    b.   Move the passenger to a shaded part of the cabin & persuade them to wear sunglasses
    c.   Move the passenger to a position where there is more sunlight
    d.   If wearing sunglasses, persuade the passenger to remove them and if necessary move to a seat nearer the C of G position

18. Which of the following is true about sleep credit/deficit:

    a.   Additional sleep can usually only be obtained when sleep credit is below maximum
    b.   Sleep deficit is not cumulative
    c.   Sleep deficit is the main factor in controlling the duration of sleep
    d.   Both credit & deficit are cumulative with no limit

19. The most effective way of analysing personality is by:

    a.   Group discussion
    b.   Interview
    c.   Written questionnaire
    d.   Practical tests

20. The risk of decompression sickness occurring in flight increases:

    a.   With a BMI less than 21
    b.   With rapid descents below 25000ft after scuba diving within 24 hours
    c.   After snorkelling followed by flight above 25000ft
    d.   After scuba diving and with age and obesity

21. The purpose of a lumbar support is to:

   a.   Allow the lower spine to curve naturally producing an even pressure on the inter-vertebral discs
   b.   Reduce back pain by straightening the spine between chest & shoulders
   c.   Keep the back straight thus reducing fatigue
   d.   Allow more curvature of the lower spinal column thus reducing pressure on the rear edges of the vertebral discs

22. Sunglasses suitable for aviation should:

   a.   Remove UV wavelengths only
   b.   Filter out the red end of the spectrum
   c.   Reduce glare by allowing only 10% of ambient light to pass
   d.   Filter out the blue and UV end of the spectrum

23. The approximate percentage of oxygen & carbon dioxide in the lungs at sea level is:

   a.   Oxygen 20%   carbon dioxide   5.5%
   b.   Oxygen 14%   carbon dioxide   5.5%
   c.   Oxygen 14%   carbon dioxide   1%
   d.   Oxygen 5.5%   carbon dioxide   14%

24. The carbon monoxide level in the blood increases with smoking and the effects of this are:

   a.   Increased apparent altitude giving better resistance to hypoxia and improved night vision
   b.   Decreased apparent altitude thus increasing the risk of hypoxia and reducing night vision
   c.   Earlier onset of hypoxia due to increased apparent altitude and reduced night vision
   d.   Later onset of hypoxia due to acclimatisation to lower oxygen levels with no effect on night vision

25. If you breathe 100% oxygen at 40000ft the partial pressure of oxygen in the lungs is:

   a.   The same as breathing 100% oxygen at 10000ft
   b.   103mm of mercury
   c.   The same as breathing air at 10000ft
   d.   The same as breathing air at sea level

26. Mental models of the external situation are:

   a.   Sometimes in error because of somatogovic illusion
   b.   Subject to the leans
   c.   Degraded by a hangover that can affect the vestibular system
   d.   All of the above

27. The effects of stress on the human being can be classified into well defined areas. Which of the following can be classified as "cognitive effects":

    a.   Headache, asthma, allergies
    b.   Forgetfulness, lack of concentration, inability to make decisions
    c.   Anxiety, depression, fatigue
    d.   Nervous laughter, trembling, neurosis

28. A handle used to open a valve should:

    a.   Always rotate in an anti-clockwise direction
    b.   Only rotate clockwise if placed in front of the pilot
    c.   Always rotate in a clockwise direction
    d.   Be clearly marked with the direction of operation in red lettering

29. The solution to spatial disorientation is for the pilot to:

    a.   Roll the aircraft in a known direction to confirm the sensations
    b.   Trust the aircraft's instruments
    c.   Look away from the instruments & to trust his own sensations
    d.   Search for visual clues

30. Which of the following is true:

    a.   An increase in age between 20-60 years is associated with slower and less accurate response
    b.   Auditory stimuli are less likely to be responded to than visual stimuli
    c.   Conditions which increase arousal levels will lead to faster but less accurate responses
    d.   Conditions which increase arousal levels will lead to faster and more accurate response

31. During visual glide slope maintenance the pilot selects an impact point on the runway & knows he is aiming at this point if:

    a.   The texture flow is parallel to the point and the visual angle between the point & the horizon increases slowly
    b.   There is no texture flow near the point & the visual angle between the point & the horizon reduces
    c.   The texture flow is away from the point & the visual angle between the point & the horizon remains constant
    d.   The texture flow is towards the point & the visual angle between the point & the horizon increases slowly

32. Rule based behaviours such as those required to fly an instrument approach are:

    a.   Stored in the short term memory
    b.   Memorised as motor programmes
    c.   Memorised by the central decision maker
    d.   Stored in the long term memory

33. Clinical insomnia is caused by:

    a.   By caffeine
    b.   By the use of valium
    c.   Adrenaline generated by mental stress
    d.   None of the above

34. The arousal mechanism operates through the:

    a.   Sympathetic nervous system that then subdues the "fight or flight" response
    b.   Automatic nervous system which controls functions over which you normally have no conscious control
    c.   The level of tolerance to environmental stress is standard across a race of people
    d.   Automatic nervous system. Once the stress source has gone, the associated energy generated into the body is immediately dissipated

35. After a loss of pressurisation cabin pressure in comparison with static pressure is likely to be:

    a.   Higher
    b.   Lower
    c.   The same
    d.   Any of the above

36. The major factor in the control of respiration is:

    a.   The level of oxygen
    b.   The apparent altitude
    c.   The level of carbon dioxide
    d.   The level of activity

37. Presbycusis is:

    a.   Noise related hearing loss
    b.   Conductive deafness
    c.   Burst eardrum
    d.   Age related hearing loss

38. After drinking residual alcohol can remain for up to 24 hours in:

    a.   The blood
    b.   The semi-circular canals
    c.   The stomach
    d.   The intestines

39. After a general anaesthetic one should not fly for:

    a.   72 hours
    b.   12 hours
    c.   24 hours
    d.   48 hours

40. Information is held in the semantic memory:

    a.   Forever
    b.   For 10-12 seconds
    c.   For 15 to 20 minutes
    d.   Until it is replaced by new inputs

HUMAN PERFORMANCE & LIMITATIONS PAPER TWO - ANSWERS

1. B	21. A
2. A	22. D
3. C	23. B
4. D	24. C
5. A	25. C
6. C	26. D
7. B	27. B
8. D	28. A
9. B	29. B
10. C	30. C
11. A	31. C
12. D	32. D
13. A	33. A
14. C	34. B
15. B	35. B
16. D	36. C
17. B	37. D
18. A	38. B
19. C	39. A
20. D	40. A

In questions 1-8 below you will be given 3 pieces of information in the following order:

i)   Lights of an another aircraft seen by you in addition to its anti-collision light
ii)   Relative bearing of the lights when first seen
iii)   Subsequent change of the relative bearing if any

Assumptions to be made:

i)   You are flying in a flying machine at night
ii)   The lights seen are those of another flying machine at about the same altitude
iii)   if avoiding action is necessary there is enough time for normal action

Answer each question from the following 4 alternatives:

(a)   There is no risk of collision
(b)   There is a collision risk, alter heading to port
(c)   There is a collision risk, alter heading to starboard
(d)   There is a collision risk, maintain heading but be prepared to take action if the other aircraft fails to give way

Notes -   (i)   "increases" or "decreases" with regard to item 3 in the question refers to the numerical change in the value of the bearing
          (ii)   where item 3 in the question is missing, no information about change in relative bearing is needed to answer that question

1.   Steady Red; 250 degrees; --------

2.   Steady Red; 060 degrees; remains constant

3.   Steady Green; 290 degrees; remains constant

4.   Steady White; 340 degrees; decreases slowly

5.   Steady Red & Green; 000 degrees; ---------

6.   Steady Green; 290 degrees; decreases quickly

7.   Steady Green & Red; 030 degrees; ---------

8.   Steady Green; 340 degrees; none

9. Within controlled airspace ATC clearance is required for:

    (a)   IFR flights at night
    (b)   All IFR flights
    (c)   VFR flights at night
    (d)   VFR flights by day or night

10. When flying on an airway on a heading of 255(M) the correct flight level will be:

    (a)   Usually ODDs
    (b)   Usually EVENs
    (c)   Always EVENs
    (d)   Always ODDs

11. En-route obstructions must be lit if they are above:

    (a)   100m agl
    (b)   150m amsl
    (c)   150m agl
    (d)   100m amsl

12. A continuous red beam directed at an aircraft from the ATC tower means:

    (a)   Airfield unserviceable, land elsewhere
    (b)   Airfield closed, do not land
    (c)   Do not land, give way to other aircraft and continue circling
    (d)   clear the landing area

13. JAR-OPS requires that the minimum crew complement that must be carried on a public transport flight is stated in:

    (a)   The Aeroplane Flight Manual
    (b)   The Air Navigation Order
    (c)   JAR Ops
    (d)   The Operations Manual

14. The take-off distance available at an airfield is made up of:

    (a)   The take-off run available plus the stopway
    (b)   The take-off run available
    (c)   The take-off run available plus the stopway plus the clearway
    (d)   the take-off run available plus the clearway

15. According to JAR-OPS standard masses for passengers can be used for the loadsheet when the number of passenger seats exceeds:

    (a)   15
    (b)   20
    (c)   30
    (d)   19

16. A public transport aircraft with 245 seats departs on a flight with a passenger load of 136. The number of flight attendants required is:

    (a)   5
    (b)   3
    (c)   6
    (d)   10

17. Public transport aircraft flying on ATS routes must be B-RNAV equipped:

    (a)   On every flight
    (b)   On any flight going out of the ECAC area
    (c)   On any flight in the ECAC area above designated levels
    (d)   On any flight within Europe

18. Following failure of two way radio communications the pilot should select one of the following on the transponder:

    (a)   Mode A 7700
    (b)   Mode A 7500
    (c)   Mode C 2000
    (d)   Mode A 7600

19. Once allocated a level to join an airway, it should be attained by:

    (a)   The airway centreline
    (b)   The airway boundary
    (c)   15nm before the airway boundary
    (d)   10nm before the airway centreline

20. The signal seen in an airfield signals square indicates:

    (a)   Both runways are in use
    (b)   The direction of take-off and landing are not the same
    (c)   Glider flying is in progress
    (d)   Light aircraft land on the grass

21. For a flight that is subject to flow management the submission time for the ATC flight plan is:

    (a)   3 hours
    (b)   30 minutes
    (c)   60 minutes
    (d)   90 minutes

22. IFR clearance is always valid:

    (a)   To the clearance limit
    (b)   For a maximum period of 5 minutes
    (c)   For a maximum period of 30 minutes
    (d)   Until landing at the destination airfield

23. If, during the descent to an airfield, the broadcast RVR is less than the specified minima the aircraft must not descend below:

  (a) 500ft
  (b) 1000ft
  (c) 3000ft
  (d) None of the above

24. During an initial climb in uncontrolled airspace, the altimeter setting should be:

  (a) The local QNH
  (b) The local QFE
  (c) The Standard Pressure Setting
  (d) Any desired value

25. A flight plan delay message must be sent after a delay of:

  (a) 1 hour
  (b) 15 minutes
  (c) 30 minutes
  (d) 2 hours

26. The obstacle clearance height relating to circling at an airfield is calculated by considering:

  (a) Aircraft type only
  (b) Obstacle height only
  (c) A minimum of 250ft clearance of obstacles
  (d) Aircraft type and obstacle height

27. With regard to SAR operations the signal seen on the ground means:

  (a) Require assistance
  (b) Require medical assistance
  (c) No assistance required
  (d) helicopter landing area

28. The controlling authority for a TMA is usually:

  (a) The ATC unit for the main airfield in the TMA
  (b) The ATCC for the FIR
  (c) The zone controller
  (d) The ATC for the airfield directly beneath the TMA

29. When approaching an airfield within a TMA the altimeter setting to be used, having passed through the transition altitude is:

  (a) Airfield QNH
  (b) Airfield QFE
  (c) Regional QNH
  (d) Regional QFE

30. Following an AIRPROX incident a report should be made:

   (a)   Immediately on landing
   (b)   Within 7 days
   (c)   Immediately by radio
   (d)   Within 24 hours

31. In Europe upper airspace begins at:

   (a)   FL 245
   (b)   FL 195
   (c)   FL 290
   (d)   Various FLs depending on country

32. Smoking is prohibited in an aircraft:

   (a)   During take-off & landing
   (b)   Whenever the Captain sees fit to forbid it
   (c)   When flying through turbulence
   (d)   At night

33. When two aircraft are approaching head on, the rules of the air require that:

   (a)   Both aircraft alter heading to starboard
   (b)   Both aircraft alter heading to port
   (c)   The larger aircraft alters heading to starboard
   (d)   The smaller aircraft alters heading to port

34. Customs airfields are:

   (a)   Open to meet regular traffic needs
   (b)   Open 24 hours
   (c)   Normally open from 0600 to 2000 UTC
   (d)   Manned only when requested

35. A pilot's flying log book should be produced, when requested by an authorised person, within:

   (a)   7 days
   (b)   24 hours
   (c)   A reasonable time
   (d)   Limits the flight to a maximum of 5nm from the nearest shore

36. The marshalling signal - "arms extended, palms facing inwards, arms swung from the extended position inwards" means:

   (a)   Stop
   (b)   Chocks inserted
   (c)   Chocks removed
   (d)   Brakes applied

37. Without special permission, the last airfield for taking off for a flight outside the EU will be:

(a) A licensed airfield
(b) Any airfield
(c) A gateway airfield
(d) A customs airfield

38. Airfield beacons at civil airfields usually show a:

(a) Two letter identification code in red
(b) Two letter identification code in green
(c) White flashing strobe light
(d) Two letter identification code in white

39. Runway visual range is reported when it falls below:

(a) 1500m
(b) 1000m
(c) 800m
(d) 1200m

40. An aircraft flying to or from abroad may cross the UK coastline:

(a) Only at a compulsory reporting point
(b) Only at a point designated on the flight plan
(c) At any point that complies with ATS routes
(d) At any point not in a prohibited area

41. The maximum permitted flight time for flight crew is:

(a) 69 hours in the 27 days prior to the flight
(b) 100 hours in the 27 days before the current flight
(c) 1000 hours in the year up to the end of the month prior to the present flight
(d) 1200 hours in the year up to the end of the month prior to the present flight

42. What flights are protected by the Prevention of Terrorism Act:

(a) Public transport flights only
(b) All flights
(c) Private flights only
(d) Military flights only

43. The problems of hijacking were discussed at:

(a) The Tokyo convention
(b) The Warsaw convention
(c) The Chicago convention
(d) The Montreal convention

44. For an aircraft registered in state A, the privilege of picking up or setting down in state B traffic destined for or which has been picked up in state C is called:

(a)   First freedom rights
(b)   Second freedom rights
(c)   Fourth freedom rights
(d)   Fifth freedom rights

45. An Instrument Rating Test is valid before renewal for:

(a)   6 months
(b)   13 months
(c)   12 months
(d)   2 years

46. The responsibility to ensure that the person loading the aircraft is suitably qualified rests with:

(a)   The airfield manager
(b)   The aircraft Captain
(c)   The aircraft operator
(d)   The loading supervisor

47. An aircraft used for simulated instrument flying must have:

(a)   A competent observer in the front seat
(b)   Dual controls
(c)   Dual controls and a competent observer
(d)   A safety pilot and dual controls

48. A danger area activated by NOTAM is shown on an aeronautical chart by:

(a)   A dashed red line
(b)   A solid red line
(c)   A solid blue line
(d)   A dashed blue line

49. The captain of a public transport aircraft must ensure that passenger seat belts are secure for:

(a)   Take-off and landing
(b)   Take-off, landing and turbulence
(c)   Take-off, landing, taxiing, turbulence & in emergencies
(d)   Take-off, landing, taxiing & turbulence

50. A UK ATPL is valid for:

(a)   Life
(b)   1 year
(c)   10 years
(d)   5 years

1. A	**26.** D
2. C	**27.** B
3. D	**28.** B
4. A	**29.** A
5. C	**30.** C
6. A	**31.** D
7. A	**32.** B
8. D	**33.** A
9. B	**34.** A
10. B	**35.** C
11. C	**36.** B
12. C	**37.** D
13. A	**38.** C
14. D	**39.** A
15. B	**40.** C
16. A	**41.** B
17. C	**42.** B
18. D	**43.** A
19. B	**44.** D
20. C	**45.** B
21. A	**46.** C
22. A	**47.** D
23. B	**48.** A
24. D	**49.** C
25. C	**50.** C

1. A series of red flashes sent to an aircraft in flight means:

   (a)   Airfield is unsafe, do not land
   (b)   Return to the airfield and land
   (c)   Give way to another aircraft and remain in the circuit
   (d)   Notwithstanding any other instructions do not land at the moment

2. An aircraft flying on airways is instructed to hold at an en-route reporting point. The correct holding procedure is:

   (a)   A right hand hold perpendicular to the airway centreline
   (b)   A right hand hold aligned with the airway centreline
   (c)   A left hand hold aligned with the airway centreline
   (d)   A left hand hold perpendicular to the airway centreline

3. If a special route forecast is required for a sector length of 450nm, the notice required by the forecast office is:

   (a)   4 hours before collection
   (b)   2 hours before collection
   (c)   2 hours before departure
   (d)   4 hours before departure

4. When viewed from the starboard side the following lights should be visible on an airship under command and making way at night:

   (a)   Anti-collision light only
   (b)   Steady green light of at least 5 candela and anti-collision light
   (c)   Steady green light of at least 5 candela, anti-collision light and a white light of at least 5 candela
   (d)   Steady green light only

5. While flying at night another aircraft reports that you are on a relative bearing of 100 degrees from him. You should see his:

   (a)   Red navigation light
   (b)   White navigation light
   (c)   Green & white navigation lights
   (d)   Green navigation light

6. One of the following statements about aircraft ground movement is correct:

   (a)   A vehicle towing an aircraft has priority over a taxiing aircraft
   (b)   Flying machines give way to vehicles towing aircraft at all times
   (c)   An aircraft overtaking another does so by passing on the right
   (d)   A taxiing aircraft has priority over a vehicle towing an aircraft

7. For an aircraft on a track of 270(M) the highest quadrantal flight level available below FL 260 is:

   (a)   FL 165
   (b)   FL 240
   (c)   FL 245
   (d)   FL 225

8. A UK registered public transport aircraft must carry two pilots if its AUW exceeds:

   (a)   2300 kg
   (b)   15000kg
   (c)   5700 lb
   (d)   5700 kg

9. A pre-flight altimeter check should be carried out:

   (a)   At the holding point
   (b)   At the runway threshold
   (c)   On the apron
   (d)   On the manoeuvring area

10. When receiving a LARS service the separation provided from known traffic will be:

    (a)   5nm
    (b)   8nm
    (c)   3nm
    (d)   3 minutes

11. A light aircraft taking off from an intermediate position on the runway after a heavy aircraft requires a wake vortex separation of:

    (a)   2 minutes
    (b)   3 minutes
    (c)   3nm
    (d)   4 minutes

12. The privilege of landing in another state for a tech stop only is:

    (a)   Second freedom rights
    (b)   First freedom rights
    (c)   Fifth freedom rights
    (d)   Third freedom rights

13. Airways normally have a lower limit that is at least:

    (a)   3000ft amsl
    (b)   FL 30
    (c)   3000ft agl
    (d)   FL 40

14. Controlled airspace is:

(a) An area within a FIR only in which an ATC service is provided
(b) An area within a FIR/UIR in which an ATC service is provided
(c) An area within a UIR only in which an ATC service is provided
(d) An area with a lower limit which is above ground level

15. When flying in advisory airspace and using an advisory service, separation is provided from:

(a) All other traffic
(b) Other known traffic
(c) Other IFR traffic
(d) Other traffic using the advisory service

16. Purple airspace is given the following ICAO classification:

(a) A
(b) D
(c) C
(d) E

17. Details of a temporary danger area will always be given in:

(a) Yellow AICs
(b) Mauve AICs
(c) NOTAMS
(d) AIP

18. If an authorised person wishes to inspect an aircraft C of A the responsibility lies with the:

(a) Commander who should produce it within 7 days
(b) Operator who should produce it within a reasonable time
(c) Operator who should produce it within 5 days
(d) Commander who should produce it within a reasonable time

19. Airfield elevation is the altitude of the:

(a) Highest point on the airfield
(b) Highest point on the landing area
(c) Highest point on the runway
(d) Lowest point on the manoeuvring area

20. EAT is the time that an aircraft:

(a) Is expected to join the hold
(b) Is expected to leave the hold and commence its approach
(c) Is expected to land
(d) Is expected to leave the last en-route holding point before destination

21. An AIRAC amendment:

(a) Is issued under the regulated System for Air Information
(b) Supersedes a previously issued NOTAM
(c) Amends the en-route section of the AIP
(d) Updates a previously issued AIC

22. In the airfield circuit the "finals" call is made when:

(a) On completion of the turn on to base leg
(b) Abeam the upwind threshold of the runway
(c) After completion of the turn on to final approach and not more than 4nm from the runway
(d) When making a straight-in approach at 6nm range

23. When only SSR is available the separation distance for traffic is:

(a) 5nm
(b) 3nm
(c) 2nm
(d) 8nm

24. An aircraft may be allowed to land on a runway before the preceding aircraft has cleared providing:

(a) That it is daylight
(b) That it is daylight and the preceding aircraft is clearly visible throughout the landing period
(c) If the runway is long enough
(d) All of the above

25. Above 30000ft the vertical separation between aircraft on reciprocal tracks will be:

(a) 2000ft
(b) 1000ft
(c) 1000ft or 2000ft depending on whether or not the aircraft are in RVSM airspace
(d) 4000ft

26. The responsibility for amending the operations manual lies with:

(a) The operator
(b) The Authority
(c) The aircraft Captain
(d) The Ground Operations Manager

27. According to JAR-OPS an operator may use his own values for standard masses of passengers as long as:

(a) The aircraft Captain is prepared to accept them
(b) An elaborate sampling procedure has been carried out and the proposed values have been submitted for approval to the Authority
(c) The values have been indicated in the Aeroplane Flight Manual
(d) The operator has indicated to the Authority that he intends to do so

28. At the correct height on the approach to a runway with PAPIs should see:

(a) Two red lights and two white
(b) Four red lights
(c) Four white lights
(d) Three white lights and one red

29. A public transport aircraft shall not take-off unless the following minima for the departure airfield are satisfactory:

(a) Cloud base and visibility
(b) Cloud ceiling and RVR
(c) Cloud base and RVR
(d) MDH and RVR

30. Under UK law the following accident is "reportable" to the Authority:

(a) An aircraft bursts a tyre on landing
(b) A passenger falls and is seriously injured while walking to the aircraft
(c) A passenger slips and is seriously injured on stairs attached to the despite aircraft being warned of the danger by a steward at the top of the stairs
(d) An attempted hijack is thwarted and the hijacker seriously injured

31. An aircraft Captain should transmit special aircraft observations when he encounters:

(a) Severe turbulence or icing
(b) Moderate turbulence, hail or Cb clouds during supersonic or transonic flight
(c) Other conditions that the Captain considers may affect the safety of other aircraft
(d) All of the above

32. On a public transport flight in a pressurised aircraft passengers must be briefed on the use of emergency oxygen:

(a) Before take-off
(b) Before climbing through FL 120
(c) Before climbing through FL 100
(d) Before climbing through FL 80

33. For a flight which requires a load sheet, one copy must be retained for:

- (a) 7 days
- (b) 14 days
- (c) 6 months
- (d) 1 month

34. Flight in search and rescue areas of operation is:

- (a) Prohibited by AICs sometimes
- (b) Prohibited sometimes by NOTAMS
- (c) Prohibited
- (d) Not prohibited

35. Aeronautical Information Circulars that deal with safety matters are:

- (a) White
- (b) Pink
- (c) Yellow
- (d) Green

36. The ICAO limit for the accuracy of VOR information on 95% of occasions is:

- (a) + or - 3 degrees by day or night
- (b) + or - 5 degrees by day only
- (c) + or - 5 degrees by day or night
- (d) + or - 3 degrees by night only

37. The maximum speed for an aircraft flying in class F or G airspace below FL 100 is:

- (a) 250 KTS IAS
- (b) 250 kts TAS
- (c) 280 kts IAS
- (d) 150 kts IAS

38. The altimeter setting for a MATZ crossing in the UK FIR is:

- (a) Airfield QNH
- (b) Regional QNH
- (c) QFE at RAF & Army airfields & QNH at RN airfields
- (d) QFE

39. With regard to flight time limitations, "flight time" means:

- (a) The total time from when an aircraft first moves under its own power for the purpose of taking off until it comes to rest after the flight
- (b) The time between take-off and landing
- (c) The time between an aircraft starting to move and coming to a complete stop plus one and a half hours
- (d) The time from crew report to 30 minutes after landing

40. Normal horizontal separation provided by radar units is:

(a) 3nm
(b) 5nm
(c) 10nm
(d) 8nm

41. With regard to declared airfield distances the Emergency Distance Available is:

(a) The distance from the start of the take-off run to the end of the clearway
(b) The distance from the start of the take-off run to the last point capable of bearing the weight
of the aircraft under normal operating conditions
(c) The distance from the start of the take-off run to the end of the stopway
(d) The area beyond the end of the prepared surface only available to aircraft stopping in an emergency

42. The holder of a flying log book must retain it for:

(a) At least 6 months from the date of the last entry
(b) 2 years from the last entry
(c) 21 days from the last entry
(d) 1 year from the date of the last entry

43. Runway thresholds at airfields listed in the UK AIP are indicated by:

(a) Green lights
(b) Red lights
(c) White lights
(d) Blue lights

44. To indicate the existence of a fuel emergency to ATC a pilot should:

(a) Request "fuel priority"
(b) Report "fuel emergency"
(c) Report "fuel state low"
(d) Declare a MAYDAY if an emergency or PAN if urgent

45. If a pilot lands at an airfield other than the destination in the flight plan he must inform the ATC unit at the original destination within:

(a) 10 minutes of the original destination ETA
(b) 45 minutes of the original destination ETA
(c) 30 minutes of the original destination ETA
(d) 60 minutes of the original destination ETA

46. A black letter "C" on a yellow background indicates:

(a) The location of ATC on an airfield
(b) The location where visiting pilots should report
(c) The location of the control tower
(d) Rest-room facilities for visiting pilots

47. Aerodrome fire and rescue category is based on:

(a) Length and weight of aircraft
(b) Length and width of aircraft
(c) Fuel load and passenger capacity of aircraft
(d) Fuel load and maximum take-off weight of aircraft

48. A tower is 3nm from an airfield and is 420ft high. Its lighting will be:

(a) Steady red lights
(b) Flashing red lights
(c) Flashing high intensity white lights
(d) Not necessary but low intensity steady red lights may be used for extra safety

49. The METAR code MIFG means:

(a) Thin fog
(b) Thick mist
(c) Shallow fog
(d) Visibility greater than 1000m but less than 1500m

50. The minimum equipment requirements for aircraft are listed in:

(a) The operations manual
(b) The UK AIP
(c) The Air Navigation (General) Regulations
(d) The Air Navigation Order

AVIATION LAW PAPER TWO - ANSWERS

1. A	26. A
2. B	27. B
3. B	28. A
4. C	29. B
5. D	30. C
6. A	31. D
7. D	32. A
8. D	33. C
9. C	34. B
10. C	35. B
11. B	36. C
12. A	37. A
13. C	38. D
14. B	39. A
15. D	40. B
16. A	41. C
17. C	42. B
18. D	43. A
19. B	44. D
20. B	45. C
21. A	46. B
22. C	47. B
23. D	48. A
24. D	49. C
25. C	50. D

1. The basic scale used by the World Meteorological Organisation for the measurement of temperature is the:

    (a)   Fahrenheit scale
    (b)   Celsius scale
    (c)   Absolute scale
    (d)   Kelvin scale

2. With reference to cloud amounts, the abbreviation BKN means:

    (a)   Between 3 & 4 oktas of scattered cloud present
    (b)   Between 1 & 2 oktas of cloud present
    (c)   The information is unreliable
    (d)   Between 5 & 7 oktas of scattered cloud present

3. The minimum temperature in the International Standard Atmosphere is:

    (a)   -273
    (b)   -100
    (c)   -56.5
    (d)   -117

4. With regard to latent heat which of the following is true:

    (a)   When water changes from a vapour to a liquid latent heat is released
    (b)   When water changes from a solid to a liquid latent heat is released
    (c)   When water changes from a vapour to a solid latent heat is absorbed
    (d)   When water changes from a solid to a vapour latent heat is released

5. Which of the following is true:

    (a)   Water vapour absorbs short-wave radiation
    (b)   The atmosphere is heated by short-wave radiation from the sun
    (c)   Water vapour and carbon dioxide absorb long-wave radiation
    (d)   Ozone allows short-wave radiation to pass through to the earth's surface

6. Ground level pressure is 1000mb and the temperature +13C. At a certain height the temperature is +10C and pressure 975mb. The value of "feet per milibar" in this atmosphere is:

    (a)   27.67 ft per mb
    (b)   29.87 ft per mb
    (c)   28.76 ft per mb
    (d)   26.76 ft per mb

7. An aircraft flying at a constant pressure altitude flies from an area of cold mean temperature to an area of warm mean temperature in the northern hemisphere. Which of the following is correct:

    (a)   The aircraft will drift to the right
    (b)   The aircraft will climb in true height
    (c)   The aircraft will descend in true height
    (d)   The aircraft will encounter a thermal tailwind

8. Which of the following is correct:

    (a)   The diurnal variation of temperature is greatest when a moderate wind is blowing
    (b)   The diurnal range of temperature sees the lowest temperature at sunrise
    (c)   The diurnal range of temperature is greatest in conditions of high humidity
    (d)   The diurnal range of temperature is least in tropical countries

9. The measurement of surface temperature is made:

    (a)   At ground level
    (b)   Approximately 10 metres above ground level
    (c)   Approximately 4 metres above ground level
    (d)   Approximately 4 feet above ground level

10. It is possible for temperature to increase with height. This is known as:

    (a)   An Inversion
    (b)   An isothermal layer
    (c)   A temperature conversion
    (d)   A steep lapse rate

11. A saturated atmosphere has a surface temperature of +12C and a temperature of +5C at 4000ft. The atmosphere is:

    (a)   Stable
    (b)   Conditionally stable
    (c)   Unstable
    (d)   Conditionally neutral

12. An aircraft is flying at FL 75 over point A where the QNH is 1013mb, en-route to B where the QNH is 979mb. Assuming that 1mb = 30ft and that the elevation of B is 823 metres, the terrain clearance over B is:

    (a)   6480ft
    (b)   3780ft
    (c)   5680ft
    (d)   7500ft

13. Pressure altitude is:

(a) The standard pressure prevailing at official airfield level
(b) The height in the standard atmosphere at which the aircraft ambient pressure would be experienced
(c) The height indicated on a pressure altimeter when the sub-scale is set to QFE
(d) The height indicated on a pressure altimeter when the sub-scale is set to QNH

14. At night the 1500ft wind, assuming no change in pressure gradient, will:

(a) Veer and increase
(b) Veer and decrease
(c) Back and decrease
(d) Back and increase

15. For a given pressure gradient the strongest wind will be the .... wind, around a .... pressure region in latitude .... The words to fill in the blanks are:

(a) Geostrophic   low   30N
(b) Gradient   high   60N
(c) Geostrophic   low   60N
(d) Gradient   high   30N

16. The moisture content or "absolute humidity" of the air refers to:

(a) Cloud
(b) Precipitation
(c) Water droplets
(d) Water vapour

17. Latent heat is defined in meterology as:

(a) The quantity of head emitted which increases the temperature of the air
(b) The quantity of heat absorbed decreasing the lapse rate of saturated air
(c) The quantity of heat absorbed which decreases the lapse rate in dry air
(d) The quantity of heat emitted which increases the lapse rate of saturated air

18. Which of the following options is the most effective way of heating the troposphere:

(a) Incoming short wave radiation from the sun
(b) Incoming long wave radiation fromt he sun
(c) Outgoing long wave radiation from the Earth
(d) Outgoing short wave radiation from the Earth

19. As air is cooled to below its dew point temperature:

(a)   The actual water vapour content increases to remain equal to the saturated water vapour content

(b)   The actual water vapour content decreases to remain equal to the saturated water vapour content

(c)   The saturated water vapour content remains constant as the air is at 100% relative humidity

(d)   The saturated water vapour content increases as precipitation takes place when the temperature drops

20. Which of the following is correct:

(a)   The Geostrophic Wind flows along straight and parallel isobars at all latitudes, except Buys Ballots Law is reversed in the southern hemisphere

(b)   The Geostrophic Force acts at 90 degrees to the isobars in equatorial latitudes

(c)   The Pressure Gradient Force acts in the same direction as the isobars in equatorial latitudes

(d)   The Pressure Gradient Force acts from High pressure to Low pressure in both hemispheres

21. The dewpoint of a sample of air is when:

(a)   Evaporation occurs

(b)   Sublimation changes the sample into water droplets

(c)   Condensation occurs

(d)   The relative humidity is 100%

22. When air is lifted due to the presence of a range of mountains in its path, the resulting vertical motion is referred to as:

(a)   Turbulence

(b)   Orographic lifting

(c)   Convergence

(d)   Frontal lifting

Appendix A is a cross section through a typical warm sector depression. Using this appendix answer the following questions.

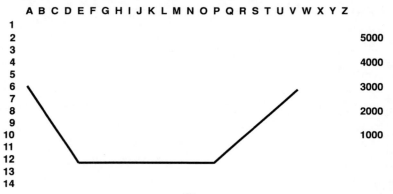

23. The base of cloud in the warm sector should be found in:

(a) Row 12
(b) Row 10
(c) Row 9
(d) Row 11

24. The precipitation in square N12 is most likely to be:

(a) Rain
(b) Showers of rain
(c) Drizzle
(d) Heavy snow showers

25. An aircraft flying in square K10 is most likely to be flying in:

(a) IMC
(b) VMC between layers
(c) VMC on top
(d) VMC with isolated showers

26. If a strong wind perpendicular to a ridge decreases or reverses in direction at medium or high levels the likely result is:

(a) Stationary rotors with very severe turbulence
(b) Travelling rotors with very severe turbulence
(c) Travelling rotors with light turbulence
(d) Stationary rotors with light turbulence

27. The start of the mature stage of a thunderstorm is identifiable from:

(a) The onset of precipitation and the "fibrous" top to the cloud
(b) Lightning
(c) Extensive light down-draughts, precipitation and lightning
(d) Very strong up-draughts & the "cauliflower" shaped top to the cloud

28. A Fohn wind is:

(a) A wind which flows down the leeside of a mountain due to its greater density
(b) A warm wind which flows down the leeside of a mountain due to the pressure distribution
(c) A dry wind which blows through a mountain gap or valley
(d) A warm dry wind which blows down the leeside of a mountain

29. Radiation fog often occurs:

(a) Near the coasts in the warm air of a polar depression in late spring
(b) In a polar low which is intensifying
(c) In anti-cyclonic conditions with air of maritime origin
(d) Along the line of a warm front of a warm sector depression

30. The intensity of precipitation associated with dense nimbostratus is:

(a)   Moderate or heavy
(b)   Light
(c)   Heavy, possibly hail
(d)   Nil

Appendix B shows four surface charts for different months of the year.
Answer the following questions with reference to the locations marked with a X.

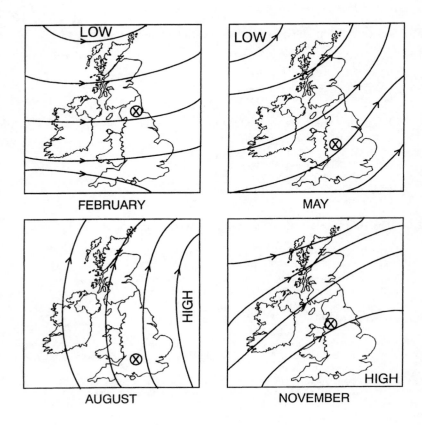

FEBRUARY

MAY

AUGUST

NOVEMBER

31. On the chart for February the airmass affecting position X is:

(a)   Tropical maritime
(b)   Polar maritime
(c)   Polar continental
(d)   Returning polar maritime

32. On the February chart the general direction of the 2000ft wind at X is:

    (a)   North easterly
    (b)   South westerly
    (c)   South easterly
    (d)   North westerly

33. On the chart for May the airmass affecting position X is:

    (a)   Polar maritime
    (b)   Tropical maritime
    (c)   Returning polar maritime
    (d)   Polar continental

34. On the August chart the airmass affecting X is;

    (a)   Tropical continental
    (b)   Polar continental
    (c)   Polar maritime
    (d)   Tropical maritime

35. In November the airmass affecting X is:

    (a)   Polar maritime
    (b)   Tropical maritime
    (c)   Returning polar maritime
    (d)   Tropical continental

36. In November the most likely weather at X is:

    (a)   Widespread stratus with drizzle
    (b)   Scattered showers
    (c)   Radiation fog
    (d)   Thunderstorms

37. A thermal depression is likely to form:

    (a)   In the lee of the Alps over northern Italy in winter
    (b)   In association with a marked trough of low pressure over the USA
    (c)   On the trailing edge of a warm sector mid latitude depression
    (d)   Over the Iberian peninsular during the summer

38. In winter mean high pressure areas appear over:

    (a)   The Aleutians, Australia, South America
    (b)   The South Pacific, The Azores, Australia
    (c)   Greenland, Siberia, NW Australia
    (d)   The Azores, The Aleutians, The South Pacific

39. Topical revolving storms usually:

    (a)   Form close to one side of the Equator and, while moving slowly in a
             westerly direction,
             cross over to the other hemisphere
    (b)   Move in a westerly direction before re-curving towards the Equator
    (c)   Do not form within 5 degrees of the Equator
    (d)   Move in an easterly direction before re-curving towards the nearest pole

40. In the disturbed temperate regions:

    (a)   The surface winds are moderate westerlies
    (b)   The weather is mainly governed by travelling frontal depressions
    (c)   The wet season is normally from May to September
    (d)   Winters are generally mild

41. The weather information passed to a landing aircraft by approach control is given in the order:

    (a)   Cloud, ceiling and RVR
    (b)   Runway in use, surface wind, visibility, weather, altimeter settings, weather
             warnings & RVR
    (c)   Cloud, surface wind, weather and visibility
    (d)   Information requested by the pilot

42. A SIGMET message concerns:

    (a)   Severe weather that is encountered by the pilot of an aircraft
    (b)   Weather conditions likely to affect the safety of aircraft operations issued by
             a local Met Office
    (c)   Weather phenomena likely to affect the safety of aircraft operations issued by a
             Meteorological Watch office
    (d)   A routine report of sig weather issued by a local Met Office

43. During an approach a head wind decreases rapidly with height as a result of windshear. If uncorrected this will result in:

    (a)   A falling airspeed and landing short of the threshold
    (b)   An increasing airspeed and landing short of the threshold
    (c)   A falling airspeed and landing upwind of the threshold
    (d)   An increasing airspeed and landing upwind of the threshold

44. With relation to isobars on the sea level chart, surface wind:

    (a)   Is inclined towards the area of low pressure
    (b)   Is inclined towards the area of high pressure
    (c)   Blows along the isobars with high pressure to the right in the northern hemisphere
    (d)   Blows along the isobars with high pressure to the left in the northern hemisphere

45. The thermal wind component:

(a) Is the resultant of the lower and upper level winds
(b) Is greatest when the temperature gradient is least
(c) Is generally weaker with a higher level or greater thickness
(d) Is generally stronger with a higher level or greater thickness

46. A source region is an area in which:

(a) Thunderstorms form or originate
(b) An air mass type forms or originates
(c) Frontal depressions form or originate
(d) Tropical revolving storms form

47. Divergence close to the surface could cause:

(a) Divergence at high level
(b) Ascent in the middle troposphere
(c) Pressure to fall at the centre of high pressure
(d) Pressure to intensify at the centre of high pressure

48. On a significant weather chart the thunderstorm symbol signifies:

(a) Moderate turbulence and moderate icing
(b) Severe turbulence and severe icing
(c) Moderate/severe turbulence and moderate/severe icing
(d) Moderate turbulence and severe icing

49. Subsidence in an anticyclone produces:

(a) Saturated air and an inversion
(b) Dry air and an inversion
(c) Isothermal dry and stable air
(d) Increased pressure at the surface

50. Frontal fog:

(a) Occurs in precipitation at a cold front
(b) Is due to evaporation of rain drops in the cold sector
(c) Is due to rain saturating the warm sector air
(d) Occurs in a narrow band where the frontal surface meets the ground

METEOROLOGY PAPER ONE - ANSWERS

1. B	26. B
2. D	27. A
3. C	28. D
4. A	29. C
5. C	30. A
6. A	31. B
7. B	32. D
8. D	33. C
9. D	34. A
10. A	35. B
11. C	36. A
12. B	37. D
13. B	38. B
14. A	39. C
15. D	40. B
16. C	41. B
17. A	42. C
18. C	43. A
19. B	44. A
20. D	45. D
21. D	46. B
22. B	47. C
23. A	48. C
24. C	49. B
25. C	50. D

1. A SIGMET is issued to aircraft in flight giving warning of phenomena on the route ahead. What distance ahead on the route does the warning cover?

   (a) 500nm or 2 hours flying time
   (b) 200nm or 1 hours flying time
   (c) 400nm or 2 hours flying time
   (d) 300nm or 1 hours flying time

2. Which of the following groups is included in a UK Terminal Aerodrome Forecast (TAF) ?

   (a) Forecast period, visibility, QNH, BECMG FM
   (b) Station identity, wind velocity, cloud, tempo
   (c) Wind velocity, cloud, RVR, BECMG AT
   (d) Forecast period, visibility, temperature, NO SIG

3. The temperature lapse rate of rising saturated air in the lower troposphere is:

   (a) 1.98 degrees C per 1000 feet
   (b) 3 degrees C per 1000 feet
   (c) 5.4 degrees C per 1000 feet
   (d) 1.5 degrees C per 1000 feet

4. The tropopause at 50N is:

   (a) Higher in the winter, lower in the summer
   (b) Lower in the winter, higher in the summer
   (c) Higher in the winter than at the Equator
   (d) Higher in the summer than at the Equator

5. Aerodrome QNH is the:

   (a) Atmospheric pressure at the aerodrome level
   (b) QFE converted to mean sea level assuming constant temperature conditions between the aerodrome and sea level
   (c) Aerodrome pressure converted to mean sea level assuming ISA conditions between the aerodrome and sea level
   (d) Lowest value of QNH forecast to occur in the region of the aerodrome during a period of one hour

6. The lowest layer of the atmosphere is heated by day by:

   (a) Conduction
   (b) Convection
   (c) Solar radiation
   (d) The release of latent heat

7. Sublimation occurs when:

(a) Air is cooled below dewpoint temperature and fog forms
(b) Water droplets in suspension condense directly into ice
(c) Water vapour in the air changes directly into ice
(d) Air is unable to support any more water vapour

8. If the relative humidity of a sample of air is 100%, then the actual amount of water vapour present would be:

(a) Greater at the poles than at the Equator
(b) Greater at the Equator than at the poles
(c) The same at the Equator as at the poles
(d) Greater at 10000ft than at mean sea level

9. An adiabatic temperature change occurs when:

(a) The air temperature is altered as pressure decreases
(b) The pressure of a parcel of air is maintained constant and the temperature is altered
(c) Air cools at 3 degrees per 1000ft
(d) No heat energy is lost or gained when a parcel of air is subjected to a change of pressure

10. Air mass thunderstorms:

(a) Tend to develop along a well marked line
(b) Have a marked diurnal variation
(c) Have a marked seasonal variation in equatorial latitudes
(d) Can give intermittent rain

11. Turbulence in the layer of the atmosphere at the earth's surface is:

(a) More severe in strong winds with an unstable atmosphere
(b) Unaffected by wind speed
(c) Unaffected by the lapse rate of temperature
(d) More severe in strong winds with a stable atmosphere

12. A ridge of high pressure is generally associated with:

(a) Divergence and subsidence causing clear skies and good weather
(b) Divergence causing cloud to break up and more precipitation
(c) Convergence causing increased cloud and precipitation
(d) Divergence causing increased cloud and precipitation

13. At an altitude of 25000ft when the temperature is -40C and the pressure is 375 mbs, the height interval corresponding to 1mb decrease in pressure is:

(a) 56ft
(b) 62ft
(c) 65ft
(d) 60ft

14. When the term INTER occurs in a trend forecast it means:

   (a)   The following intermediate conditions apply
   (b)   Changes are expected to last for a period of less than 1 hour in each instant
   (c)   Changes are expected to occur frequently for short periods of time
   (d)   A change is expected to occur in a short period of time

15. Low cloud in temperate climates, excluding heap, are those existing from:

   (a)   1000ft to 6500ft
   (b)   The surface to 7500ft
   (c)   The surface to 6500ft
   (d)   The surface to 7500 metres

16. Uneven heating of a land surface by day in a stable atmosphere is most likely to form:

   (a)   Stratocumulus cloud
   (b)   Fair weather cumulus cloud
   (c)   Alto cumulus castellanus
   (d)   Fracto stratus cloud

17. Over the British Isles a returning polar maritime airmass would have:

   (a)   Latent instability
   (b)   Stability
   (c)   Instability
   (d)   Potential instability

18. Intensity of precipitation is described as:

   (a)   Intermittent, continuous or showery
   (b)   Slight, moderate or heavy
   (c)   Intermittent, moderate or heavy
   (d)   Drizzle, rain or snow

19. Stratus cloud of limited depth at a temperature of -5C will most likely give:

   (a)   Moderate to heavy rime ice
   (b)   Light to moderate glaze ice
   (c)   Moderate to heavy glaze ice
   (d)   Light to moderate rime ice

20. The situation where rain ice is likely to occur must be avoided. This would be when flying:

   (a)   In the warm sector of a frontal depression during winter
   (b)   Through an active cold front
   (c)   Ahead of a warm front with the OAT gauge reading -5C
   (d)   In a polar maritime airstream behind a cold front

21. Frontal fog is most likely to:

(a) Form ahead of a vigorous fast moving cold front
(b) Form ahead of a warm front
(c) Form on a vigorous cold front and last for many hours
(d) Form to the rear of a warm front but only last for 1 to 2 hours

22. Two factors which contribute to the formation of radiation fog are:

(a) A high relative humidity and clear night skies
(b) A high relative humidity and no wind
(c) Clear night skies and a low relative humidity
(d) A light wind (5 to 8 knots) and good cloud cover

23. The force which causes the air to flow parallel to the curved isobars is called:

(a) Centrifugal force
(b) Geostrophic force
(c) Gradient force
(d) Cyclostrophic force

24. A katabatic wind is a wind which:

(a) Flows down a hill or mountain during the night
(b) Flows up a hill or mountain during the day
(c) Flows up a hill or mountain during the night
(d) Flows down a hill or mountain during the day

25. The thermal wind component is:

(a) Generally stronger with a higher level or greater thickness
(b) The resultant of the lower level wind and the upper level wind
(c) Greatest when the temperature gradient is least
(d) Generally weaker with a higher level or greater thickness

26. Typically a Jet Stream is:

(a) 1000nm long, 150nm wide and 5nm deep
(b) 1000nm or more long, 5000ft to 10000ft wide & 1000ft deep
(c) 1000nm long, 150nm wide and 5000ft to 10000ft deep
(d) 150nm long, 500nm wide and 5000ft deep

27. Which of the following is true:

(a) Only the SW monsoon affecting the west coast of India is very moist and stable
(b) The monsoon low of India causes the SE trades which have crossed the Equator to form the SW monsoon to turn left in the Bay of Bengal to affect the coast of India
(c) In winter the "Crachin" affecting Hong Kong is due to the SE monsoon
(d) The NE monsoon is due to the inflow of air into the large low pressure area of India

28. In July light easterly upper winds are apparent:

(a) All along the Equator
(b) At 20N over Asia and Northern Africa
(c) 10S
(d) 20N to 05S over the Pacific Ocean

29. Which of the following statements about the ITCZ is correct?

(a) Its associated weather is invariably strong convergence and heavy cumuliform cloud
(b) Its furthest displacement from the Equator is normally about 45S
(c) It is normally fed with converging northern and southern trade winds
(d) In the southern summer it is normally positioned entirely south of the Equator

30. Which of the following statements is correct?

(a) The easterly jet stream normally appears at the 200mb level
(b) In winter the Savannah climatic region is governed by the equatorial rains
(c) Trade winds seldom extend much above 5000ft
(d) The outflow of air from the Siberian high over northern China and Japan is initially northwesterly

Using the Frankfurt Sig weather chart and wind & temperature charts for FL 300 and FL 340 at Annex A answer the following questions.

31. Which of the following is the is the most likely AVERAGE wind velocity on a flight from OSLO (6010N 1105E) to Zurich (4725N 0835E) at FL 300?

(a) 285(T)/65
(b) 280(T)/45
(c) 310(T)/60
(d) 270(T)/40

32. On the same flight as above the cloud that can be expected is:

(a) Overcast layered cloud from below FL 100 to FL 320
(b) 5 to 7 octas layered cloud from below FL 150 to FL 320
(c) 5 to 7 octas layered cloud from below FL 100 to FL 260
(d) Overcast layered cloud from below FL 150 to FL 320

33. The height of the tropopause on this leg averages:

(a) 34000ft
(b) 45000ft
(c) 30000ft
(d) 39000ft

34. A depression is approaching the route to Zurich; it is moving at:

(a)   Slow, less than 5 knots
(b)   10 knots
(c)   15 knots
(d)   20 knots

35. The height of the freezing level overhead Athens is:

(a)   FL 100
(b)   1300ft
(c)   Fl 130
(d)   Below FL 130

36. The average temperature on a flight from Zurich to Athens at FL 340 is:

(a)   -45C
(b)   -48C
(c)   -50C
(d)   -44C

Use the following airfield forecast to answer questions 37 & 38

LSZH 1019 20018G30KT 9999 RA SCT050 BKN080 TEMPO 1015 23012KT
6000 -DZ BKN015 BKN030 BECMG 1518 23020G35KT 4000 RA OVC010 =

37. What is the forecast weather for the period 1800 - 1900 UTC?

(a)   Rain
(b)   Light drizzle
(c)   + rain and intermittent drizzle
(d)   - rain and continuous drizzle

38. The forecast visibility for the period 1200 - 1500 UTC is:

(a)   More than 10km, temporarily 6000m
(b)   More than 10km becoming 4000m
(c)   More than 10km becoming 6000m
(d)   6000m becoming 4000m

39. In a polar maritime airstream the surface wind at midnight compared to the surface wind at midday has:

(a)   Veered and increased
(b)   Backed and increased
(c)   Veered and decreased
(d)   Backed and decreased

40. A microburst associated with a CB cloud will normally occur:

    (a)   From a point mid-way up in the cloud
    (b)   Anywhere up to 10 miles ahead of the cloud
    (c)   Near the base of the cloud
    (d)   Only ahead of the surface impact point

41. In the mature phase of a thunderstorm's development:

    (a)   Strong updraughts predominate
    (b)   The storm is dying out
    (c)   The anvil top spreads out
    (d)   Precipitation begins

42. In temperature latitudes frontal thunderstorms:

    (a)   Persist longer than airmass thunderstorms
    (b)   Have a large diurnal variation in summer
    (c)   Have a marked seasonal variation
    (d)   Have a large diurnal variation in winter

43. The magnitude of the Geostophic Force:

    (a)   Increases with decrease of wind speed
    (b)   Is not affected by the windspeed
    (c)   Increases with increase of wind speed
    (d)   Decreases with an increase of latitude

44. Turbulence cloud describes a cloud that is:

    (a)   Associated with moderate or severe turbulence
    (b)   Often associated with CAT
    (c)   Stratiform and extends, at low level, over large areas
    (d)   Stratiform and extends, at low level, over a large area of land only

45. Hail occurs when:

    (a)   Water vapour changes directly into ice
    (b)   Supercooled water droplets freeze
    (c)   Rain drops freeze on falling from a CB
    (d)   Snowflakes melt and then re-freeze

46. A microburst associated with a CB clound will normally occur:

    (a)   Near the base of the cloud
    (b)   From a point mid-way up in the cloud
    (c)   Anywhere up to 10 miles ahead of the cloud
    (d)   Only ahead of the surface impact point

47. The Sirocco occurs:

(a) Due to intense heating causing convectional dust storms
(b) Due to the steep temperature gradient along the N. African coast
(c) Behind a frontal depression moving east along the coast
(d) Ahead of a frontal depression moving east along the coast

48. Sumatras are associated with:

(a) Arch shaped banks of CBs
(b) Torrential rain and a very sharp windshear
(c) A marked rise in day time temperature
(d) A marked fall in daytime temperature

49. The wind which results from the warming on the side of a valley is known as:

(a) A fohn wind
(b) A katabatic wind
(c) An anabatic wind
(d) A valley wind

50. Which of the following best describes the first stage of development of a sea breeze:

(a) Pressure initially falls at height over land
(b) Warm air rises over land so cold air moves in from the sea to replace it
(c) Pressure initially falls at the surface over the sea
(d) Pressure intially rises at height over the land

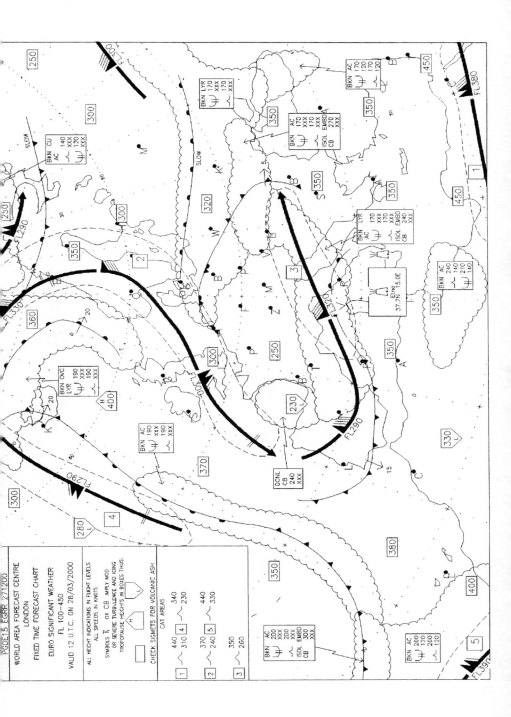

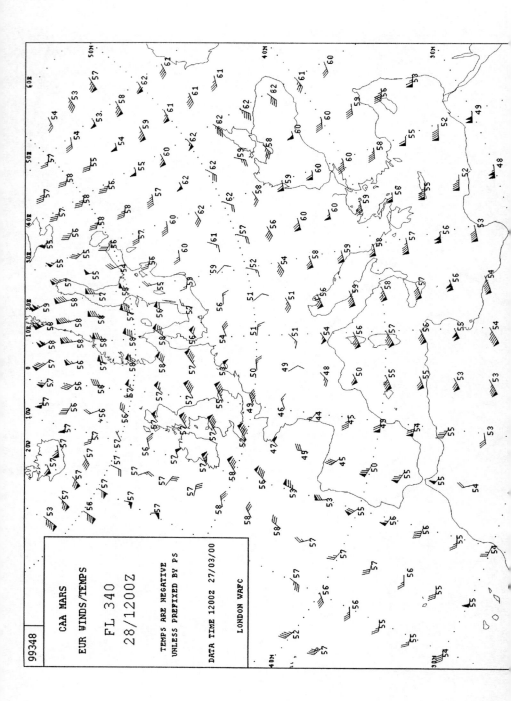

CAA MARS
EUR WINDS/TEMPS
FL 340
28/1200Z

TEMPS ARE NEGATIVE
UNLESS PREFIXED BY PS

DATA TIME 1200Z 27/03/00

LONDON WAFC

99348

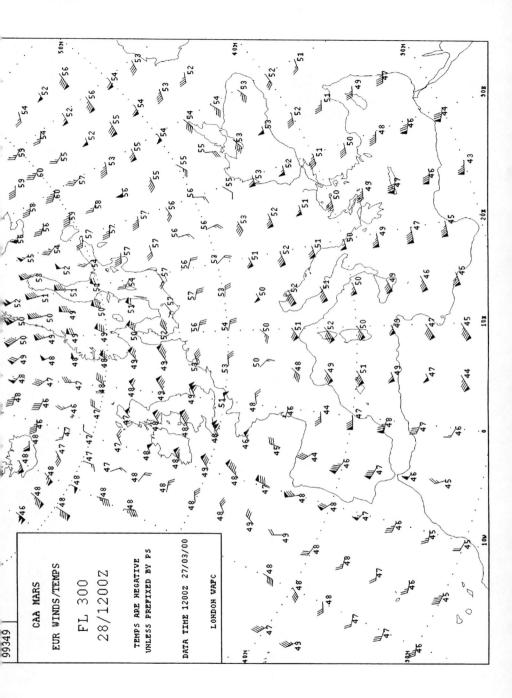

CAA MARS
EUR WINDS/TEMPS

FL 300
28/1200Z

TEMPS ARE NEGATIVE
UNLESS PREFIXED BY PS

DATA TIME 1200Z 27/03/00

LONDON WAFC

99349

METEROLOGY - PAPER TWO - ANSWERS

1. A	26. C
2. B	27. B
3. D	28. B
4. B	29. C
5. C	30. D
6. A	31. B
7. C	32. A
8. B	33. C
9. D	34. D
10. B	35. C
11. A	36. B
12. A	37. A
13. D	38. A
14. C	39. D
15. C	40. C
16. B	41. D
17. A	42. A
18. B	43. C
19. D	44. C
20. C	45. B
21. B	46. A
22. A	47. D
23. D	48. B
24. A	49. C
25. A	50. D

1. When tuning in an NDB:

    (a)   The BFO must always be switched on
    (b)   The ADF selector must be on
    (c)   The ANT or SENSE switch must be on
    (d)   The Bandwidth selector must be off

2. With regard to ADF which of the following is correct:

    (a)   The range is directly proportional to the square root of the power output
    (b)   Range can be increased by increasing frequency
    (c)   To double the range the power must be increased twofold
    (d)   Range is inversely proportional to the cube root of the power input

3. With ADF which of the following is correct:

    (a)   Promulgated range is the area within which accuracy of the system is guaranteed
    (b)   A daylight range of 450nm will be reduced to about 70nm at night
    (c)   The promulgated range is valid throughout the day and night
    (d)   The protection range guarantees an accuracy of + or - 5 degrees within the service area

4. An aircraft on a heading of 235(M) obtains a RMI bearing of 090 degrees from an NDB. Any quadrantal error which is affecting the accuracy of this bearing is likely to be:

    (a)   Zero, since quadrantal error does not affect the RMI
    (b)   A very small value
    (c)   Zero, since quadrantal error affects only the RBI
    (d)   A maximum value

5. The reference signal from a VOR is:

    (a)   Amplitude modulated
    (b)   Phase modulated
    (c)   Frequency measured
    (d)   Frequency modulated

6. The warning flag on an O.B.I. will be activated:

    (a)   When overhead the VOR station
    (b)   When abeam the VOR with a radial selected
    (c)   When the aircraft is out of range of the beacon
    (d)   When the VOR monitor detects a change of radial bearing of half a degree

7. The measured phase difference in a VOR receiver when the aircraft is on a QDR of 149(T) with a local variation of 14E is:

   (a)   149 degrees
   (b)   163 degrees
   (c)   135 degrees
   (d)   329 degrees

8. The maximum theoretical range to be expected from a VOR situated 735ft amsl when the aircraft is flying at 23000ft is:

   (a)   223nm
   (b)   179nm
   (c)   313nm
   (d)   206nm

9. The principal advantage of a doppler VOR is that:

   (a)   The effective range is increased
   (b)   The DOC is valid both day and night
   (c)   Site errors are considerably reduced
   (d)   Transmitter frequency instability is minimised

10. With reference to a VOR a radial is:

   (a)   Magnetic bearing from the VOR
   (b)   True bearing from the VOR
   (c)   Magnetic bearing to the VOR
   (d)   Relative bearing of the beacon from the aircraft

11. Frequency paired VOR and DME installations are:

   (a)   Always co-located
   (b)   Able to be at different locations
   (c)   Either co-located or associated
   (d)   Always associated

12. The delay incorporated in the ground transponder of a DME is:

   (a)   100 microseconds
   (b)   25 microseconds
   (c)   There is no delay in the ground transponder
   (d)   50 microseconds

13. The accuracy of a measured DME slant range will be:

   (a)   + or - 1% of range or 1nm whichever is greater
   (b)   + or - 3% of range or 1nm whichever is greater
   (c)   + or - 3% of range or 1/2 nm whichever is greater
   (d)   + or - 1% of range or 1/2 nm whichever is greater

14. Secondary radars transmit and receive on two different frequencies which helps to:

(a) Eliminate weather interference
(b) Measure accurately phase difference
(c) Measure accurately the frequency difference
(d) Prevent self triggering

15. Mode "A" SSR reply from an aircraft is;

(a) A random code transmission used to identify a primary radar return
(b) An allocated code transmission used to identify a primary radar return
(c) A coded transmission giving height information based on the aircraft's altimeter sub-scale setting
(d) A code transmission giving the pressure height of the aircraft based on a datum level of 1013.2 mbs

16. The special identification pulse in SSR keyed in by the aircraft's crew indicates:

(a) An emergency
(b) A positive identification of the aircraft's primary radar return
(c) A hijack
(d) Control and eradication of any false lobe interrogation

17. The vertical coverage of the safe pattern extends up to:

(a) 7 degrees
(b) 9 degrees
(c) 8 degrees
(d) 6 degrees

18. What height is the ILS reference datum where the Glide Slope aerial is situated 300m upwind from the ILS threshold and the glide slope angle is 2.75 degrees:

(a) 55 feet
(b) 65 feet
(c) 45 feet
(d) 60 feet

19. What is the characteristic identification of an ILS outer marker:

(a) White light - dots   - high tone
(b) Blue light   - dashes   - low tone
(c) White light - dashes   - high tone
(d) Amber light - dots/dashes - low tone

20. What is the angular coverage of the ILS localiser at a range of 18nm:

(a)   8 degrees either side of the runway centreline
(b)   25 degrees either side of the runway centreline
(c)   35 degrees either side of the runway centreline
(d)   10 degrees either side of the runway centreline

21. An SRA radar with a high resolution capability can give guidance in an approach to a runway; this guidance in azimuth will terminate at:

(a)   1nm
(b)   2nm
(c)   3/4 nm
(d)   1/2 nm

22. An area guidance radar operating on a 30cm wavelength will have an operational range of approximately:

(a)   250 nms
(b)   100 nms
(c)   150 nms
(d)   400 nms

23. Airborne weather radars are generally based on the use of:

(a)   Primary radar in the UHF band
(b)   Secondary radar in the SHF band
(c)   Primary radar in the SHF band
(d)   Secondary radar in the VHF band

24. What would be the approximate minimum range for using the pencil beam in mapping mode with the AWR:

(a)   7 - 100 nms
(b)   50 - 60 nms
(c)   100 - 120 nms
(d)   40 - 50 nms

25. The main factor which affects the maximum range of radar is the:

(a)   Radio frequency of transmission
(b)   Size of the radar screen
(c)   PRF
(d)   Size of the aerial system

26. With regard to the AWR, to prevent the ground returns cluttering the cloud returns, the .... must be adjusted:

(a)   Tilt
(b)   Gain
(c)   Brilliance
(d)   Focus

27. The "Height Ring" on an AWR screen is:

    (a)   Useful in giving an accurate aircraft height
    (b)   Caused by the side lobes of the radar beam
    (c)   Useful for terrain avoidance calculations
    (d)   Caused by tilting the beam downwards

28. A positive doppler shift is occasioned when:

    (a)   The receiver is moving away from a stationary transmitter
    (b)   The transmitter is moving away from a stationary receiver
    (c)   A transmitter and a receiver are moving apart
    (d)   The transmitter is moving towards a stationary receiver

29. "Sea movement" error in a doppler system is caused by:

    (a)   The differing temperatures of layers of salt water
    (b)   The movement of the surface of the water
    (c)   The different densities of layers of salt water
    (d)   A calm sea surface inducing loss of energy from the front of the beam

30. The doppler memory circuit will operate when the returned "signal to noise" ratio drops below a ratio of:

    (a)   7 to 1
    (b)   10 to 1
    (c)   2 to 1
    (d)   5 to 1

RADIO NAVIGATION PAPER ONE - ANSWERS

1. C	16. B
2. A	17. A
3. B	18. C
4. D	19. B
5. B	20. D
6. C	21. D
7. C	22. A
8. A	23. C
9. D	24. B
10. A	25. C
11. B	26. A
12. D	27. B
13. C	28. D
14. D	29. B
15. B	30. C

RADIO NAVIGATION - PAPER TWO

1. A hyperbolic position line is defined as:

    (a) A line joining points of equal phase
    (b) A line joining all points of equal difference of distance between two fixed points
    (c) A line which cuts the base line between two stations at 90 degrees
    (d) A conic section

2. The range of Decca by day is:

    (a) 300nm
    (b) 150nm-200nm
    (c) 200nm
    (d) 600nm

3. Before flight OMEGA navigation equipment requires the following inputs:

    (a) Start position and initial track
    (b) UTC time, UTC date and required station selection
    (c) Start position and required station selection
    (d) Start position, UTC time and date

4. The decca navigation system works on the principle of:

    (a) Pulsed time comparison
    (b) Phase comparison of the slave signals against an atomic time standard
    (c) Phase comparison of both master and slave signals against an atomic time standard
    (d) Differential range by phase comparison

5. In a hyperbolic navigation system the risk of fixing ambiguity exists:

    (a) Close to the right bisector
    (b) Close to the base line
    (c) Close to the base line extensions
    (d) At extreme range

6. Omega is a network of .... transmitting stations located throughout the world to provide world-wide coverage:

    (a) 6
    (b) 8
    (c) 10
    (d) 12

7. To avoid modal interference Omega stations are deselected when the range from the aircraft to the transmitter drops below:

   (a) 800nm
   (b) 600nm
   (c) 400nm
   (d) 500nm

8. With regard to ADF the which of the following is correct:

   (a) The RBI bearings are true bearings
   (b) Static presents no problem with ADF closed loop detection systems
   (c) The RBI shows QDMs towards the NDB station
   (d) Frequency bands are upper LF and lower MF

9. Coastal refraction is caused by:

   (a) Bending of radio waves caused by tropospheric scatter
   (b) Bending of radio waves caused by wet, salty conditions
   (c) Bending caused by differing speeds of travel over different surfaces
   (d) Bending of radio waves by Ionospheric refraction

10. Two ways of minimising coastal refraction are:

    (a) Take the bearing at 90 degrees to the coast and from inland beacons
    (b) Take the bearing only during the day and from coastal beacons
    (c) Take the bearing parallel to the coast and from inland beacons
    (d) Take the bearing at 90 degrees to the coast and from coastal beacons

11. Ground Direction Finding is limited by regulation to:

    (a) 25nm and 10000ft on approach frequencies
    (b) 25nm and 10000ft on tower frequencies
    (c) 25nm and 4000ft on approach frequencies
    (d) 10nm and 4000ft on tower frequencies

12. The Designated Operational Coverage (DOC) of a VOR station is:

    (a) A volume of airspace within which interference is avoided
    (b) Published in NOTAMS
    (c) Valid during daylight only
    (d) The range from a VOR station where interference from another VOR
        (on the same frequency) is avoided

13. An aircraft flies over position A through the true North of a VOR station at position B. The magnetic variations are 22W at A and 15W at B. The aircraft is on radial:

    (a) 022 degrees
    (b) 015 degrees
    (c) 345 degrees
    (d) 338 degrees

14. The following is a significant error of VOR:

    (a)   Night effect
    (b)   Static error
    (c)   Site error
    (d)   Coastal refraction

15. While using a VOR the ident stops but bearings are still displayed. This means:

    (a)   The station is on test and must not be used
    (b)   The transmitter's battery is over the time limit
    (c)   The station is on test but can be used with caution
    (d)   The transmitter's error has become unacceptable

16. The bearing actually measured by the VOR receiver is equal to the aircraft's:

    (a)   QDR
    (b)   QUJ
    (c)   QDM
    (d)   QTE

17. When DME is used in association with ILS the DME range is to:

    (a)   The DME station
    (b)   The ILS threshold
    (c)   The ILS localiser
    (d)   The aerodrome datum

18. With regard to ILS which of the following is correct:

    (a)   On a five dot instrument, each dot represents 0.4 degrees
    (b)   The modulation designation of the marker beacons is NONA2A
    (c)   The maximum safe deviation below the glide slope is shown as 2.5 dots fly up
    (d)   The frequency of the ILS localiser is in the UHF band

19. Assuming an ILS reference datum of 60ft and a glide slope of 3 degrees, at 6nm on the approach the aircraft will be at a height AGL of:

    (a)   1900ft
    (b)   2060ft
    (c)   1960ft
    (d)   1720ft

20. A VHF signal is transmitted from an aircraft at FL 230. It will first be received by an aircraft at FL50 when the aircraft are:

    (a)   210 nms apart
    (b)   164 nms apart
    (c)   227 nms apart
    (d)   278 nms apart

21. If a DME ground transmitter fails:

(a) All pilots immediately lose range information
(b) The last measured range is displayed for about 10 seconds before unlock occurs
(c) The last measured range is re-computed until the ground transmitter restarts
(d) None of these

22. Assuming the normal accuracy limits of DME a range indication of 150nm would mean that the aircraft's range was between:

(a) 154.5nm and 145.5nm
(b) 153nm and 157nm
(c) 151.5nm and 158.5nm
(d) 156nm and 144nm

23. The final letter of the three letter designator of a DME beacon is "Z". This indicates that:

(a) The DME is co-located with a VOR
(b) The DME is not associated with a VOR but both serve the same location and may be used in connection
(c) The DME is associated with a VOR
(d) The DME is not co-located or associated with a VOR

24. "Fruiting" is when:

(a) Two aircraft in close proximity reply together causing interference to both reply transmission chains
(b) Interference to the airborne transmission chain is caused by weather
(c) An aircraft is interrogated simultaneously by more than one SSR radar
(d) Interference to the airborne transmission chain is caused by another transmitter

25. In the event of an emergency which of the following should be selected on the airborne SSR:

(a) A 7500
(b) A 7600
(c) A 7000
(d) A 7700

26. Maximum doppler shift in frequency will occur:

(a) From a reflecting surface directly ahead of the aircraft
(b) From a reflecting surface directly beneath the aircraft
(c) From a reflecting surface illuminated by a beam transmitted at approximately 70 degrees depression angle to the aircraft's horizontal axis
(d) From a reflecting surface illuminated by a beam transmitted at approximately 60 degrees depression angle to the aircraft's horizontal axis

27. Incorrect setting of the doppler land/sea switch when an aircraft is over the sea will cause:

(a)   Errors in drift indications
(b)   An under reading of ground speed
(c)   An over reading of ground speed
(d)   No error in ground speed indication

28. In a doppler derived position indicator the greatest contribution to error is:

(a)   The across track error due to lower doppler components than the along track components
(b)   The uncertainty of the value of the sea movement error
(c)   The compass input
(d)   Prolonged use of the land/sea switch over a near calm sea

29. Hill shadow effect:

(a)   Shows up as false stretches of water on the radar when flying over forested plains
(b)   Is caused by screening of the transmitted radar signals
(c)   Is caused by screening of the transmitted radar signals
(d)   Is caused by uni-directional icing of the aerial dish

30. According to JAR fixed reference symbols on Electronic Flight Instrument systems (EFIS) are coloured:

(a)   Red
(b)   Green
(c)   Blue
(d)   White

1. B	16. A
2. A	17. B
3. D	18. C
4. D	19. C
5. C	20. D
6. B	21. B
7. B	22. A
8. D	23. B
9. C	24. C
10. D	25. D
11. A	26. A
12. A	27. B
13. B	28. C
14. C	29. C
15. D	30. D

1. An aircraft load sheet should be retained for:

    (a)   3 months
    (b)   6 months
    (c)   2 years
    (d)   12 months

2. An operator of Public Transport aircraft must maintain a library of documentation relevant to his operations. This will include NOTAMS:

    (a)   Always
    (b)   Only if Class II NOTAMS are not available
    (c)   Unless he is satisfied that they are always available from the local AIS unit when required
    (d)   When 24 hour company operations cover is not available

3. Detailed guide lines for the information to be presented in Operations manuals are contained in:

    (a)   Both JAR-OPS & CAP 360
    (b)   CAP 360
    (c)   JAR-OPS
    (d)   The Air Navigation Order

4. An Operator has an aircraft licensed in the Transport Category (Passenger). The Operator wishes to use the aircraft for carrying cargo and so must:

    (a)   Apply to the authority for a variation of the C of A
    (b)   Apply to the authority for a variation of the AOC
    (c)   Revise the Operations Manual and have it approved by the authority
    (d)   Take no action

5. Following an accident, the operator of an aircraft on which a flight recorder is carried shall preserve recorded data pertinent to that accident for a period of:

    (a)   30 days
    (b)   1 year
    (c)   6 months
    (d)   60 days

6. For aircraft with a maximum certificated take-off mass of 5,700kg or more, the flight data recorder shall be capable of retaining the data recorded during at least the last .... hours of its operation:

    (a)   12 hours
    (b)   25 hours
    (c)   48 hours
    (d)   6 hours

7. Applications for variations to an AOC must be submitted at least ...... days before the date of intended operation except that the Operations Manual may be submitted later but not less than ...... before the date of intended operation:

(a)   60   and   30
(b)   90   and   60
(c)   90   and   30
(d)   60   and   15

8. Unless specifically approved by the authority an operator shall not operate a two-engined aircraft with a MTOM in excess of 8618kg further from an adequate airfield than the distance flown in .... minutes at the one-engine-inoperative cruise speed:

(a)   60
(b)   90
(c)   120
(d)   138

9. The time in question 8 above is known as the:

(a)   Rule Time
(b)   ETOPS segment
(c)   Threshold time
(d)   Threshold distance

10. Areas suitable for break-in by rescue crews in emergency shall be marked:

(a)   Red
(b)   Yellow
(c)   Red or Yellow
(d)   White

11. Which of the following have a considerable effect on braking capability:

(a)   Tyre tread, runway contamination and runway surface
(b)   Runway surface, brake type and take-off speed
(c)   Runway surface, surface wind and tyre diameter
(d)   Tyre tread, brake type and tyre diameter

12. If an item not on the MEL is unserviceable, the aircraft may be operated for Public Transport providing:

(a)   A licensed engineer signs the necessary Certificate of Release to Service
(b)   A licensed engineer considers it safe to operate and the Captain is satisfied that it will be safe to do so
(c)   The operation without this item of equipment is specifically authorised by JAR-OPS
(d)   The aircraft operator authorises the operation

13. The dangerous goods transport document regarding the safe transport of dangerous goods by air is included in:

    (a)   Operations manual
    (b)   Flight manual
    (c)   Certificate of Airworthiness
    (d)   Technical Instructions

14. The vertical limits of MNPS airspace are:

    (a)   FL 285 to FL 420
    (b)   FL 330 to FL 370
    (c)   FL 285 to FL 390
    (d)   FL 310 to FL 420

15. It is recommended that Oceanic clearance is obtained .... minutes before the Oceanic entry point:

    (a)   30
    (b)   40
    (c)   10
    (d)   20

16. An Operational Flight Plan is to be prepared and used:

    (a)   For all flights
    (b)   For all IFR flights
    (c)   For all flights other than those intended to take-off land at the same aerodrome
    (d)   For all international flights

17. If meteorological or performance reasons prevent an aircraft from returning to the departure airfield in the event of an emergency after take-off, an operator of two-engined aircraft must select a take-off alternate within:

    (a)   60 mins
    (b)   120 mins
    (c)   30 mins
    (d)   1 hour at the one engine inoperative cruising speed according to the AFM

18. With regard to the selection of destination alternates, the operator shall only select aerodromes where the weather conditions will be at or above the planning minima during the period:

    (a)   1 hour before ETA until 3 hours after ETA
    (b)   3 hours before ETA until 3 hours after ETA
    (c)   From ETA until 1 hour after ETA
    (d)   From 1 hour before ETA until 1 hour after ETA

19. A commander shall ensure that flight crew members engaged in performing duties essential to the safe operation of an aircraft use supplemental oxygen whenever:

(a)   Cabin altitude exceeds 10000ft
(b)   Cabin altitude exceeds 13000ft
(c)   Cabin altitude exceeds 8000ft
(d)   Cabin altitude exceeds 10000ft for a period in excess of 10 minutes

20. On a non-precision approach, unless the required visual reference has been established, descent is not permitted below:

(a)   MDA/H
(b)   DA/H
(c)   200ft
(d)   1000ft

21. An operator shall ensure that a pilot does not operate as pilot-in-command unless:

(a)   He holds a valid Airline Transport Pilots Licence
(b)   He holds a valid Instrument rating
(c)   He has completed a minimum of 3 take-offs and 3 landings as pilot flying in the preceeding
       90 days in either an aeroplane or approved flight simulator of the type to be used
(d)   All of the above

22. With regard to additional crew members who are not required flight or cabin crew members an operator shall ensure that:

(a)   They have been trained in, and are proficient to perform, their assigned duties
(b)   They receive a full passenger safety briefing
(c)   They are have received some first aid training
(d)   None of the above

23. An operator is allowed to use an aircraft with certain items of equipment unservicable if this is provided for in:

(a)   The Operations Manual
(b)   The Aircraft Flight Manual
(c)   The Minimum Equipment List within the Operating Manual
(d)   The Maintenance Schedule, in the Approval Specifications Section

24. Which of the following prohibit a crew member from performing his/her duties

(a)   While taking any medication
(b)   Following blood donation unless a reasonable time period has elapsed
(c)   When alcohol has been consumed within 12 hours of the flight
(d)   When not fully acclimatised to a different time zone to that of his/her base

25. Which of the following combinations of documents must be carried on every flight:

(a) Certificate of Airworthiness, Air Operator Certificate, Air Navigation Order
(b) Air Operator Certificate, Aircraft Radio Licence, Certificate of Registration
(c) Aircraft Radio Licence, Tecnical Log, Maintenance Schedule
(d) Certificate of Airworthiness, Flight Time Limitations, AFM

26. With regard to Leasing, a "Wet Lease" is:

(a) Where the aircraft is operated under the AOC of and with crew provided by the lessee
(b) Where the aircraft is operated under the AOC of the lessee but with crew provided by the lessor
(c) Where the aircraft is operated under the AOC of the lessor but with crew provided by the lessee
(d) Where the aircraft is operated under the AOC of and with crew provided by the lessor

27. A Fail Operational flight control system is:

(a) A system that includes an automatic landing system
(b) A flight control system that, in the event of a failure, there is no significant out-of-trim condition or deviation of flight path or attitude but the landing is not completed automatically
(c) A flight control system that, in the event of a failure below alert height, the approach, flare and landing can be completed automatically
(d) A system which consists of a primary fail-passive automatic landing system and a secondary independent guidance system

28. Operators shall not conduct Category II or III operations unless:

(a) The flight crew consists of at least 2 pilots
(b) The operations are approved by the authority
(c) Each aircraft concerned is certificated for operations with decision heights below 200ft or no decision height, and equipped in accordance with JAR-AWO or an equivalent accepted by the authority
(d) All of the above are satisfied

29. The minimum visibility and separation from cloud for VFR is:

(a) 5km, clear of cloud and in sight of the surface in all classes of airspace
(b) 5km below 10000ft and 1000ft vertically in all classes of airspace except class G
(c) 8km below 10000ft and 1000ft horizontally in all classes of airspace except class G
(d) 5km and 1500ft horizontally in class G airspace

30. Special VFR flights must not be commenced when the visibilty is less than:

(a) 3km
(b) 1.5km
(c) 8km
(d) 5km

OPERATIONAL PROCEDURES PAPER 1 - ANSWERS

1. B	**16.** C
2. C	**17.** D
3. A	**18.** D
4. D	**19.** B
5. D	**20.** A
6. B	**21.** D
7. B	**22.** A
8. A	**23.** C
9. C	**24.** B
10. C	**25.** B
11. A	**26.** D
12. B	**27.** C
13. D	**28.** D
14. A	**29.** B
15. B	**30.** A

1.   For a runway to be considered as contaminated which of the following
        percentages of the surface area (whether in isolated areas or not) within
        the required length and width being used is covered:

        (a)   25%
        (b)   50%
        (c)   More than 25%
        (d)   15%

2.   With regard to circuit protection devices, an operator shall not operate an
        aeroplane in which fuses are used unless there are spare fuses available for
        use in flight equal to at least .... of the number of fuses of each rating or
        .... of each rating whichever is the greater:

        (a)   10% and   3
        (b)   10% and   5
        (c)   5% and 10
        (d)   5% and   3

3.   The carriage of airborne weather radar is mandatory at night in
        pressurised aircraft:

        (a)   Which have a maximum certificated take-off mass of more than 5700kg
        (b)   Which have a maximum approved passenger seating configuration of more
                than 9 seats
        (c)   In IMC
        (d)   At all times

4.   In general terms a crew member interphone system is required in
        aircraft with:

        (a)   Maximum certificated take-off mass in excess of 5700kg
        (b)   Maximum certificated take-off mass in excess of 15000kg or a maximum
                approved seating configuration of more than 19
        (c)   Maximum certificated take-off mass in excess of 15000kg or a maximum
                approved seating configuration of more than 9
        (c)   Maximum approved seating configuration of more than 9

5.   For aircraft with a maximum certificated take-off mass in excess of 5700kg
        the cockpit voice recorder shall be capable of retaining information
        recorded during at least:

        (a)   The last 2 hours of its operation
        (b)   The last 30 minutes of its operation
        (c)   The last 60 minutes of its operation
        (d)   Its entire flight

6. A door between the passenger compartment and the flight deck compartment with a "crew only" placard and a locking means is required:

    (a)   On all public transport aircraft
    (b)   On aircraft with a maximum approved passenger seating configuration of more than 19
    (c)   On aircraft with a maximum certificated take-off mass in excess of 5700kg
    (d)   On all pressurised aircraft

7. For an aircraft with 150 seats installed the minimum number of first aid kits required is:

    (a)   1
    (b)   3
    (c)   4
    (d)   2

8. A audio selector panel which is accessible to to each required crew member is required when an aircraft is operating:

    (a)   Under VFR
    (b)   On all flights
    (c)   Under IFR
    (d)   On public transport flights

9. For flights operating under IFR or under VFR over routes not navigated by reference to visual landmarks which of the following combinations of communication and navigation equipment satisfies the requirements of JAR-OPS:

    (a)   One VOR, one ADF, one DME, one Marker Beacon receiving system and two independent radio communication systems
    (a)   one VOR, one ADF, one DME and two independent radio communication systems
    (c)   Two VOR, one ADF, one DME and one radio communication system
    (d)   Two VOR, two DME and two independent radio communication systems

10. A pre-flight inspection is:

    (a)   An inspection carried out before the aircraft's maiden flight
    (b)   An inspection carried out before flight to ensure that the aircraft is fit for the intended flight and which does not include defect rectification
    (c)   An inspection carried out before flight to ensure that the aircraft is fit for the intended flight and which includes defect rectification
    (d)   A check of the aircraft's technical log carried out by a JAR-145 organisation

11. The aircraft technical log must be retained for:

    (a)   12 months after the date of the last entry
    (b)   6 months after the date of the last entry
    (c)   3 months after thedate of the last entry

12. Notwithstanding an operator's responsibilities pursuant to the Air Navigation Order for an aerodrome to be considered "adequate" it should be expected that at the anticipated time of use:

    (a)   The aerodrome will be available and equipped with necessary ancilliary services and at least one letdown aid will be available for an instrument approach
    (b)   The runway available will be sufficient for the aircraft to land
    (c)   The runway will be of sufficient length and have at least one precision approach aid
    (d)   The aerodrome will be available and equipped with necessary ancilliary services

13. A "Suitable" aerodrome is:

    (a)   An aerodrome which has engineering support for the aircraft type in operation
    (b)   An "adequate" aerodrome where, at the anticipated time of use, the weather conditions are very likely to be at or above the normal operating minima at the time of the intended operation
    (c)   An "adequate" aerodrome with engineering support for the aircraft type in operation
    (d)   An en-route alternate that will be open during the intended time of operation

14. An ETOPS segment is:

    (a)   The whole of an ETOPS flight
    (b)   The portion of an ETOPS flight that begins when the aircraft is first more than threshold distance from any adequate aerodrome and ends when it is last more than threshold distance from any adequate aerodrome
    (c)   The portion of an ETOPS flight that begins when the aircraft is first more than the rule distance from any adequate aerodrome and ends when it is last more than rule distance from any adequate aerodrome
    (d)   The portion of an ETOPS flight that begins when the aircraft is first more than thresh old distance from any suitable aerodrome and ends when it is last more than threshold distance from any suitable aerodrome

15. With regard to aircraft in Performance Class B an operator shall not operate a single-engine aeroplane:

    (a)   At night
    (b)   In IMC
    (c)   At night or in IMC except under Special VFR
    (d)   In IMC except under Special VFR

16. The maximum distance of a take-off alternate is:

    (a)   2 hours flight time at a one engine inoperative cruising speed in still air conditions based on actual take-off mass for 3 & 4 engined aeroplanes
    (b)   2 hours flight time at a one engine inoperative cruising speed for 2 engined aeroplanes
    (c)   1 hours flight time at a one engine inoperative cruising speed for 2 engined aeroplanes that have been authorised for ETOPS
    (d)   1 hours flight time at a one engine inoperative cruising speed for 3 & 4 engined aeroplanes

17. A destination alternate need not be selected if:

  (a)   The duration of the planned flight does not exceed 6 hours
  (b)   Two separate runways are available at the destination
  (c)   Two separate runways are available at the destination and the meteorological conditions will allow an approach from the relevant minimum sector altitude and landing in VMC
  (d)   The duration of the planned flight does not exceed 6 hours and two separate runways are available at the destination and prevailing meteorological conditions from 1 hour before until 1 hour after ETA will allow the approach from the relevant minimum sector altitude and landing to be made in VMC

18. An operator must select two destination alternates:

  (a)   When no meteorological information is available
  (b)   When the destination is isolated
  (c)   When the nearest suitable alternate does not have a precision approach aid
  (d)   When the nearest suitable airfield does not have 24 hour customs cover

19. The landing mass of an aeroplane in Performance Class A must be such as to allow a full stop landing from 50ft above the threshold:

  (a)   Within the whole of the landing distance available
  (b)   Within 60% of the landing distance available for turbopropeller powered aeroplanes
  (c)   Within 70% of the landing distance available for turbojet powered aeroplanes
  (d)   Within 60% of the landing distance available for turbojet powered aeroplanes

20. If, when operating within North Atlantic Airspace an aircraft is unable to continue the flight in accordance with its ATC clearance:

  (a)   The aircraft should set heading immediately for the nearest alternate aerodrome
  (b)   Until a revised clearance is obtained the specified NAT in-flight contingency procedures should be carefully followed
  (c)   The aircraft should commence a descent immediately to leave the Organised Track System
  (d)   The aircraft should return to its departure airfield

21. The general concept of NAT in flight contingency procedures is:

  (a)   Offset from the assigned route by 30nm and climb or descend to a level which differs from those normally used by 500ft if below FL 410 or by 1000ft if above FL 410
  (b)   To enable an aircraft to divert as quickly as possible
  (c)   To enable an aircraft to descend as quickly as possible
  (d)   To enable aircraft to continue to destination in the event of an in-flight emergency

22. If an aircraft is carrying out the NAT contingency procedures and, once established on the offset track, can maintain its assigned flight level, the subsequent action is:

  (a)   Climb or descend 1000ft if above FL 410
  (b)   Climb or descend 500ft if above FL 410
  (c)   Climb or descend 1000ft if below FL 410
  (d)   Maintain assigned FL

23. With regard to the Organised Track System (OTS) in the NAT region:

(a) The day-time OTS is valid between 1130 UTC and 1800 UTC at 20W
(b) The west bound OTS is valid between 0100 UTC and 0800 UTC at 30W
(c) The night-time OTS is valid between 1130 UTC and 1800 UTC at 30W
(d) The east bound OTS is valid between 0100 UTC and 0800 UTC at 30W

24. Preferred Route Messages (PRMs) should be submitted:

(a) 1000 UTC for the following day-time OTS
(b) 1900 UTC for the following night-time OTS
(c) 1000 UTC for the following night-time OTS
(d) 0100 UTC for the following day-time OTS

25. Which of the following should be planned between significant points

(a) Rhumb line track
(b) Minimum time track
(c) Minimum distance track
(d) Great circle track

26. Aircraft flying in the NAT region should operate transponders continuously:

(a) Mode A/C 7700
(b) The last assigned domestic code for 30 mins after entry into NAT airspace and then Mode A/C 2000
(c) The last assigned domestic code
(d) Mode A/C 2000

27. For an aircraft with a maximum approved passenger seating configuration of 363 the minimum number of hand fire extinguishers to be located in the passenger compartment(s) is:

(a) 4
(b) 7
(c) 5
(d) 3

28. Above what figure for maximum approved passenger seating configuration must an additional crash axe or crowbar be carried:

(a) 250
(b) 150
(c) 100
(d) 200

29. Above what maximum certificated take-off mass is an aircraft to be to fall in the "heavy" wake turbulence category

(a)   136,000kg
(b)   136,000lb
(c)   15500lb
(d)   300,000kg

30. If a "heavy" aircraft is landing after another "heavy" aircraft, the recommended separation is:

(a)   5nm
(b)   4nm
(c)   2 minutes
(d)   8nm

OPERATIONAL PROCEDURES PAPER 2 - ANSWERS

1. C	**16.** A
2. A	**17.** D
3. D	**18.** A
4. B	**19.** C
5. A	**20.** B
6. B	**21.** A
7. D	**22.** A
8. C	**23.** D
9. A	**24.** C
10. B	**25.** D
11. D	**26.** B
12. A	**27.** C
13. B	**28.** D
14. B	**29.** A
15. C	**30.** B

1.   What is the correct way for requesting QFE?

(a)   Request Quebec Fox Echo
(b)   Request Quebec Farm Echo
(c)   Request Quebec Foxtrot Echo
(d)   Request Queen Foxtrot Easy

2.   On the readability scale, readability 3 means:

(a)   Readable
(b)   Perfectly readable
(c)   Readable now and then
(d)   Readable with difficulty

3.   An aircraft may use an abbreviated callsign:

(a)   Once it has been addressed in this manner by the ground station
(b)   Only in VFR conditions
(c)   Only if a flight plan has been filed
(d)   Once satisfactory communication has been established and there is no chance of confusion

4.   If an error is made in a transmission the pilot should:

(a)   Use the words "I say again" and repeat the whole message
(b)   Use the word "Correction", repeat the last correct word or phrase and continue
(c)   Use the word "Correction" and repeat the whole message
(d)   Use the words "I say again" and repeat the last correct word or phrase and then continue

5.   In radio telepheny the number 3500 should be transmitted as:

(a)   Three thousand five hundred
(b)   Three five zero zero
(c)   Thirty five hundred
(d)   Three five hundred

6.   The frequency 128.725 MHz should be transmitted as:

(a)   One two eight decimal seven two five
(b)   Two eight decimal seven two five
(c)   One two eight decimal seven two
(d)   One two eight seven two five

7.   The word "STANDBY" means:

(a)   Wait to be called
(b)   Continue as filed and wait for further instructions
(c)   Change frequency and listen out
(d)   Secondary frequency

8. The standard word to indicate agreement is:

(a) Yes
(b) Roger
(c) Affirm
(d) Affirmative

9. The word "ROGER" means:

(a) Your last message has been received
(b) Your last message has been received and understood
(c) Your last message has been received and I am complying with your instructions
(d) I am changing frequency

10. With regard to the categories of radio telephony message which of the following lists is correct in terms of priority (in descending order):

(a) Urgency, Distress, Communications related to direction finding
(b) Distress, Urgency, Communications related to direction finding
(c) Distress, Urgency, Flight Safety messages
(d) Urgency, Flight Safety messages, Meteorological messages

11. URGENCY is defined as:

(a) A condition of being threatened by serious and/or imminent danger and of requiring immediate assistance
(b) A condition concerning the safety of your aircraft and requiring immediate assistance
(c) A condition concerning the safety of an aircraft or other vehicle or some person on board or within sight but which does not require immediate assistance
(d) A condition of emergency

12. The correct address for a ground station at Bristol providing approach control would be:

(a) Bristol Approach
(b) Bristol Approach Control
(c) Bristol Radar
(d) Bristol Ground

13. If an aircraft transmits a message preceeded by the phrase "Transmitting blind due to receiver failure" the aircraft station shall also:

(a) Proceed to the alternate airport
(b) Repeat the whole message
(c) Enter the nearest en-route holding pattern
(d) repeat the whole message and advise time of next transmission

14. In the event of failure of two-way communications failure, the transponder (if fitted) should be set to:

    (a)   Mode A/3 code 7700
    (b)   Mode A/3 code 7500
    (c)   Mode A/3 code 2000
    (d)   Mode A/3 code 7600

15. In the event of two-way communications failure in VMC the correct procedure is to:

    (a)   Continue to fly in VMC
    (b)   Continue to fly VMC and land at the nearest suitable aerodrome
    (c)   Land at the nearest suitable aerodrome
    (d)   Continue the flight as planned

16. In the event of two-way communications failure in IMC which of the following is one of the ICAO required procedures:

    (a)   Land within 60 minutes of the ETA on the filed flight plan
    (b)   Proceed to the nearest suitable alternate aerodrome
    (c)   Proceed as current flight plan to the appropriate designated navigational aid serving the aerodrome of intended landing and when required hold over this aid until commencement of descent
    (d)   Transmit blind and wait for another aircraft to relay for you

17. The term "aeronautical station" means:

    (a)   A station in the aeronautical mobile service located on land or, in certain circumstances, on board a ship or a platform at sea
    (b)   An airborne station forming part of the aeronautical fixed telecommunication network (AFTN)
    (c)   Any station established to exchange messages
    (d)   A station in the aeronautical telecommunication service that is to be found on an aircraft or on land to exchange R/T communications

18. The international distress frequency is:

    (a)   121.5 MHz
    (b)   243.0 KHz
    (c)   121.5 KHz
    (d)   2182 Hz

19. The range of frequencies in the VHF band is:

    (a)   118 to 136.975 Khz
    (b)   118 to 136.975 Hz
    (c)   118 to 136.975 MHz

20. If a controller answering a distress message asks the pilot to use the speechless code and he responds by pressing his transmit button for three short transmissions, this means:

(a)   Affirmative
(b)   Say again
(c)   Negative
(d)   Roger

COMMUNICATIONS - ANSWERS

1. C
2. D
3. A
4. B
5. B
6. C
7. A
8. D
9. A
10. B
11. C
12. A
13. D
14. D
15. B
16. C
17. A
18. A
19. C
20. B